EXODUS

STOP WALKING IN CIRCLES

BIBLE STUDY | 6 LESSONS

REBECCA BENDER

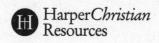

HarperChristian
Resources

Exodus
© 2022 by Rebecca Bender

Requests for information should be addressed to:
HarperChristian Resources, 3900 Sparks Dr. SE, Grand Rapids, Michigan 49546

ISBN 978-0-310-14106-8 (softcover)
ISBN 978-0-310-14107-5 (ebook)

All Scripture quotations, unless otherwise noted, are taken from the Holy Bible, New International Version®, NIV®. Copyright © 1973, 1978, 1984, 2011 by Biblica, Inc.® Used by permission. All rights reserved worldwide.

Scripture quotations marked AMP are taken from the Amplified® Bible. Copyright © 1954, 1958, 1962, 1964, 1965, 1987 by The Lockman Foundation. Used by permission. www.Lockman.org.

Scripture quotations marked ESV are taken from the ESV® Bible (The Holy Bible, English Standard Version®). Copyright © 2001 by Crossway, a publishing ministry of Good News Publishers. Used by permission. All rights reserved.

Scripture quotations marked KJV are taken from the King James Version. Public domain.

Scripture quotations marked MSG [or The Message] are taken from *The Message*. Copyright © Eugene H. Peterson 1993, 1994, 1995, 1996, 2000, 2001, 2002. Used by permission of NavPress. All rights reserved. Represented by Tyndale House Publishers, Inc.

Scripture quotations marked NLT are taken from the Holy Bible, New Living Translation, copyright © 1996, 2004, 2015 by Tyndale House Foundation. Used by permission of Tyndale House Publishers, Inc., Carol Stream, Illinois 60188. All rights reserved.

Any internet addresses (websites, blogs, etc.) and telephone numbers in this study guide are offered as a resource. They are not intended in any way to be or imply an endorsement by HarperChristian Resources, nor does HarperChristian Resources vouch for the content of these sites and numbers for the life of this study guide.

HarperChristian Resources titles may be purchased in bulk for church, business, fundraising, or ministry use. For information, please e-mail ResourceSpecialist@ChurchSource.com.

Cover design: Ron Huizinga
Cover photo: Prystai / Shutterstock
Interior typesetting: Kait Lamphere

First Printing December 2021 / Printed in the United States of America

To my Nannie Phyllis, you have prayed me through and are a constant reminder of what is good and true. I am here because of the promises God made you.

CONTENTS

A MESSAGE FROM REBECCA

I WASN'T RAISED IN CHURCH, quite the contrary, I grew up in a broken home riddled with substance abuse and mental health issues, absent of much hope. I found myself a full-blown addict at the age of 21 standing outside a rehab days before Christmas in 2002, smoking menthols, high as a kite, listening to a former gang member lead me through the "sinner's prayer" so I could go inside and get sober. I'd intentionally avoided faith-based rehabs because of the judgments and dismissals I'd experienced from people in the church.

Yet, somehow, it was in that rehab, full of drug addicts, people in prostitution and gang members, where the string of moments when I'd almost died in life, were all highlighted as second chances. Where I just knew I was being given another shot—from something or someone way bigger than this world.

I was given the Bible in rehab, and I started learning how to contextualize what I read so it made sense to me and *my* life. I fell in the love with the first five books of the Bible because the people were just as messed up as I was, and I could relate to their struggles. But please note, my experience still tells me to be careful of religiosity—it didn't go so well for some people in the Bible either.

After I got a taste of freedom in the words and stories I read, I still went back to a violent man who I thought I could change with my new "bippity boppity boo" idea of how God answers prayer. What a misguided understanding I still carried. I had no clue what exploitation and human trafficking was back then, and I underestimated what it looked like to break out of true mental chains and cycles of abuse modeled through generations before me. I just thought I was in domestic violence and that prostitution was "our hustle." I knew of freedom; it just wasn't fully mine yet.

See, no matter what bondage any of us has ever experienced—super extreme, TV-mini-series worthy, within our mind of comparison and devaluation, or literally anywhere in between—we are still walking in circles until we stop and make the choice to focus, change our habits, and accept the help we are offered. Not one of us can claim a day or week without a nasty thought or angry feeling, so let's not pretend.

We can ALL relate to the feeling of being trapped. Trapped in toxic habits, in dead-end jobs, ugly pasts, uglier presents, in unfulfilling relationships, in mental chains of envy, bitterness, anger, pride, or selfish ambition. It's *all* stopping us from reaching our true destinies.

Whatever past you come from; you have promises waiting for you in Christ. You are not alone—I want to reach the promises that God has for me also. I keep walking in circles, too, friend, failing test after test, trial after trial. Truth is there is nothing any of us can do that hasn't been done, and God guarantees He is *still* for us and won't let us go until we believe it. So, let's dig in together, breaking habits that maybe we don't even know we have, and reach our promised land.

—Rebecca Bender

INTRODUCTION

EACH OF US HAS HABITS and hang-ups that can sometimes stop us from getting a promotion, hurt our relationships with those closest to us, or stunt our growth toward deeper levels of intimacy.

You know who God is calling you to be but sometimes wonder how you are ever going to get there. If you knew what was holding you back, then you'd fix it and be there already, right? This journey through Exodus is designed to give you some tools to help you break those bad habits and move you into your promised land, the place God is calling you to.

Exodus has 40 chapters we could explore, and I encourage you to do that. But this is a study on purpose and destiny, so we will be focusing more specifically on the beginning five chapters, and then twelve through thirty-two. Believe me when I say we could do an entire Bible study just on Moses, or just on the burning bush, or any other of the many gold nuggets in this fabulous book. For our journey together, we're going to stay focused. Take your time and read each suggested passage to give yourself a clear understanding of the context that we will further explore.

Remember this: The God that freed you from addiction can free you from gossip. The God that moved you away from abuse can move you away from a critical spirit. The God that brought you back to life can bring you into your destiny. The God who seems to be silent, or is not where you thought he'd be, is working and leading you still. You don't have to walk in circles hoping for more, longing for deeper connections with purpose and passion. He has a plan for your life and intends to see you reach it just like He intended the children of Israel to reach Canaan, a land flowing with milk and honey. Just like them, we have to break some habits along the way in order to develop our character so we can sustain the calling we are moving into.

REMEMBER THE PROMISE

STEAM ROSE from the Manhattan sidewalk as Crystal heaved her red suitcase from the back seat of the taxi. The car lurched forward. "Wait!" she called, as she snatched her purse from the back seat. The driver hit the gas and the heavy door slammed shut. Mud and bits of gravel flew past as Crystal backed up, her stiletto heel teetering near a grate in the sidewalk. She could already feel rain streaking down the back of her neck and soaking her shirt. She pulled her newest copy of the *Perinatal Journal* from her purse and held it over her head while she searched for numbers on the building that would tell her she was in the right place. As the newest doctor at the city's top labor and delivery hospital, she was desperate to make a good impression.

She needed to clean up and drop her suitcase in her new apartment before she headed to the office. She recognized the address above a gleaming glass door in the building behind her and made a run for it. Ducking inside, she glanced over at the doorman, wiping a drip from her chin and fumbling for her keys. "Hi," she smiled breathlessly. "I'm Dr. Smith, the new tenant in 802. Nice weather y'all are having." He scowled at the puddle forming under her feet and went back to scrolling on his phone. Not quite the southern charm Crystal was used to. "This should be fun," she mumbled as she pushed the elevator button for the eighth floor.

Now, let me paint this picture for you another way:

Rain splattered through the opening of the dirty canvas on the covered wagon, but Crystal was too tired to tie it shut again. She squished her toes around inside her drenched leather shoes and hugged her bag close to her chest. Hopefully at least some of her books and instruments wouldn't be damaged beyond repair. She leaned forward and peeked out at the main street of Denver, Colorado. It was lined with wagon tracks and slick with steaming mud. Rough wooden sidewalks tottered on each side of the crowded street. The sun peeked from behind the clouds, glaring off the dirty glass windows of the local saloon. Crystal tried to remind herself why she was at it again, relocating her one-woman show to Denver to follow her passion for midwifery. A woman helping women deliver babies: Why was this such a hard concept for people? She wiped her face and tried to smooth her hair as the wagon lurched to a stop. "This should be fun," Crystal mumbled as she gathered her skirt and stepped over the side of the wagon.

SETTING MATTERS

A seminary professor once said that if you do not have the context—the setting—you're trying to understand a conversation by reading only one side of a text message.

Setting paints a picture that unlocks clues about a character and what they want. Subtle descriptions about environment or appearance can lead us to important points of the story that we could miss without understanding the setting.

If you're anything like me, you probably pictured every step Crystal Smith took as I described them. Each tiny detail offers clues as to who the woman is, what her interests are, and a bit of her background. With these nuggets, we might be able to anticipate what lies ahead for her. What did you imagine differently about Crystal's character when we switched from modern-day Manhattan to the early nineteenth century of the American West? What types of problems might she have encountered in muddy

Colorado versus New York City? How do we think of options and opportunities available to her when we compare these two time periods?

Time periods, eras, surroundings, buildings, roads, and characters all play a major role in helping us better understand a storyline. This is especially true when we are studying the Bible. Setting and context can help us interpret what the writers are telling us in this ancient and still living God-breathed text.

THE CONTEXT OF EXODUS

I would be remiss to start our study without diving into the setting of Exodus. We are going to use the inductive study method—a fancy way to say Who, What, Where, When, Why, and How—which will help us to better interpret what is happening, where our lives collide with the text, and how we can apply the same lessons learned by those thousands of years ago today.

"In our modern world, we have cultural nuances that we have come to know and understand. These consist of various ideas and ways of thinking such as natural rights, freedom, capitalism, democracy, individualism, globalism, postcolonialism, postmodernism, market economy, scientific naturalism, an expanding universe, empiricism, and natural laws, just to name a few. Though many of these are seen in the United States, these concepts are known and flow around the globe and affect many cultures. In the ancient world, we saw varying community groups: Egyptians, Hittites, Phoenicians, Canaanites, Armenians, Assyrians, Babylonians, and Israelites. And despite the variations among cultures and across the centuries certain elements remained static. Some of these cultural nuances include community identity, the comprehensive and ubiquitous control of the gods, the role of kingship, divination, the centrality of the temple, the mediatory role of images, the reality of the spirit world and magic, and the movement of the celestial bodies is the communication of the gods. If we want to understand what the Bible is teaching, we have to know what the ancient cognitive environment was, in the same way that if we want to know what the Bible is saying we have to be able to read Hebrew. This is what we mean when we say the cultural cognitive environment must be translated."[1]

The children of Israel were enslaved for 400 years—20 generations of people. Think about that for a moment. Do you have any knowledge of your own lineage 20 generations back? These people had not only forgotten the promises God made to their forefathers, but their circumstances and culture were inherently ignorant of the character of God, how good He was and how much He had in store for them. This is not far off from us today. Sometimes we need a reminder of the promises of God while we are living in a culture that can muddy and cloud our understanding. As we do a deeper dive into Exodus, I trust that the Holy Spirit will help you recognize your own setting, your own history, and your own forgotten promises. May you learn to lean in and hear Him so you can prepare for what is ahead.

Several years ago, I was speaking at a local church in my hometown. A girl I had gotten in trouble with during high school was in the audience. She had been suspended for fighting a few times, and we both had babies out of high school. I knew her brother was in jail for selling drugs. After I shared my testimony that Sunday, we started talking in the lobby.

"I didn't know you had been through all of that after school," she said, raising her eyebrows.

"Ya, pretty crazy!" I laughed.

"I'm glad I came today." She nodded, focusing her eyes intently on her feet.

"I show up at church every now and then . . ." she said softly, her attention now shifting around the room. "I hear the pastor from the stage and it's not bad—it's fine. But I know he doesn't get it."

Her eyes finally looked into mine.

"He doesn't understand the struggle of lives like ours," she said. I could see the heartache in her eyes.

She was right. Many people, myself included, sit in Sunday morning chairs and we hear what can come across like cliché Scriptures being thrown around like coffee mug mantras. Or maybe under all the performative displays we still aren't getting a heart encounter with the creator of the universe. Either way, we go home and believe we're the only ones not getting it because we *"don't hear Him like that"* or *"we come with too much baggage to sort through."*

But the reality is none of that is true. You have a promise and a call from God regardless of your past. You DO hear from God—we all do. How you hear from Him might be different from someone else and different in each season, but we all hear Him. When we press in, when we put it on the calendar to seek Him, when we wade through our endless to-do lists and racing thoughts, we will find more direction and purpose than we could ever hope for or imagine. Our "hearing," like all muscles when being exercised, gets stronger.

I promise you, friend, when you have a true encounter with God, you cannot help but be transformed. This week, may you simply be open to whatever He has for you.

MONDAY

Inheritance

Have you ever sat and wondered, *How did I get here?* Or better yet, *Where am I going next?*

I sat in my bedroom early one morning trying to focus on prayer. While my kids and husband got ready downstairs, I was determined to make this my new "war room" where I did spiritual battle for my family, but I was getting nothing. I tried to journal; I read parts of the Bible; I turned on worship music. I tried standing, then sitting, then laying down. Still nothing. What once was easy—ushering in the presence of God—seemed harder and harder. Thoughts, anxiety, and to-do lists crowded my mind. I felt lost without a map.

This went on for a few weeks. Some days I'd just sit and weep with no real words. I was discouraged and emotionally exhausted and needed God's direction more than ever.

It was an incredibly challenging time in my life for many reasons and my frustration was piqued by how the absence of God in the way I thought I needed him felt. It was a season. A hard, lonely, difficult season. You know the one? It feels more like a Grand Canyon-sized chasm, and you wonder how you'll ever move on. When in the past you've sensed gentle nods from the Lord or highlights from the Holy Spirit in prayer, now you hear nothing but echoes of your own questions .

How about the seasons without any real "destination," with no idea of the future or what God has in store? In the midst of these seasons, our culture seems to shout self-focused motivational sayings. Social media influencers pitch us tweetable lines, and every day there just seems to be less to admire or imitate and more to question. Our world is more advanced than ever before, more dazzling than it has ever been. We have more technology, more buildings, more money, more population, more glitz . . . more, more, more. And yet in every season we have fewer answers, less direction, and a growing sense of emptiness.

This is not so different from the Egyptian culture where we find the children of Israel when God starts calling them into their next season. When our story picks up, the great pyramid of Giza and the iconic sphinx were already twenty-five-hundred years old! Egypt was a dazzling, iconic civilization that flourished with professions and beauty and travel. It was New York meets Los Angeles meets Las Vegas—a metropolitan mecca. The center for trade and commerce, art, and education of its time.

The children of Israel were completely removed from the promises of their forefathers. They were enveloped in the rituals, social behavior, beliefs, laws, customs, and habits of the Egyptian culture. And maybe like you, they needed a little reminder of the promises received from God generations prior. Maybe they needed a reminder of that promise from their twenties that they thought they got wrong. Or maybe they needed to be reminded of that thing, when they were little, that they used to daydream about and play about before life settled in and daily items piled up so high that those dreams were dismissed as "child's play." Maybe they needed a reminder of what God had promised their parents or their grandparents as inheritance and what they were leaving their kids.

The Beginning of a Great Nation
READ EXODUS 1:1-7

> [1] *"These are the names of the sons of Israel who came to Egypt with Jacob, each with his family:* [2] *Ruben, Simeon, Levi, and Judah,* [3] *Issachar, Zebulun, and Benjamin,* [4] *Dan and Naftali, Gad and Asher.* [5] *All the descendants of Jacob numbered seventy in all; Joseph was already in Egypt.* [6] *Now Joseph and all his brothers and all that generation died,* [7] *but the Israelites were fruitful and multiplied greatly and became exceedingly numerous, so that the land was filled with them."*

We pick up in Exodus 1:1, 400 years after the end of Genesis. Joseph has died after serving as Pharaoh's second-in-command and the Hebrew civilization is fully settled in Egypt. Let's take a quick recap of what happened to get us to this moment:

- Abraham is the father of the faith, through whom God has chosen to bring forth the Messiah. In Genesis 12:2–3, we are introduced to the plan of salvation through the Abrahamic Covenant. Through Abraham and Sarah, the Chaldeans emerge in modern-day southern Iraq. They move to Canaan, and God makes His promise: He is going to make Abraham into a great nation, blessing him, and making his name great. He will bless those who bless Abraham and curse those who curse him.
- Abraham, Isaac, and Jacob carry the promise. Eventually, Jacob's son Joseph and his entire family are living in Egypt with Joseph working as second only to Pharaoh. They are given the land of Goshen, and 73 people live there. After 400 years, about 20 generations, the Hebrews in Goshen have multiplied and filled the land.

Before we continue, let me address the Pharaohs. There are more than eleven Pharaohs who ruled during the oppression of the Hebrews and the period of Exodus. However, throughout this study, you will see at least three Pharaohs who are central to our story: one who ruled while Joseph served, one who ruled over the childhood of Moses, and a third who ruled throughout the plagues and the return of Moses. Scholars are unclear about which Pharaoh may have been in charge during each specific timeframe, but we have some guesses. Regardless, it is helpful to recognize that we are dealing with at least three different demigod Pharaohs as we consider the context of our story.

Also, the exact time period of the Exodus is under constant debate by scholars due to a variety of evidence found that aligns with varying parts of the narrative text. But for this study we're going to stick to the years between 1300–1250 BC which puts Rameses II as the Pharaoh at the time.

Keep that in mind as you read, because not only does the setting matter, but our context is crucial as well. I have a friend who posted a beautiful picture of him and his wife and their four children on Instagram. I wept. I wept because I know that several years prior, his first wife, the biological mother of those children, died a tragic death. The wife in this picture had stepped in, not to replace, but to love and support. This photo takes on a whole new meaning when you have the backstory.

Exodus is one of the most fundamental books of Christianity and Judeo belief systems. It is THE entire book on which our spiritual heritage rests. It contains the Ten Commandments and the basis for how God creates His own people into a holy nation. The children of Israel, from whom Jewish heritage comes, is birthed out of this moment in Exodus when Hebrew slaves are delivered and formed into a nation. It is the foundation for so many of the additional stories we find in the Bible: Rahab, judges, kings, and priests who come from the tribe of Levi. These details depict how the children of Israel went from Hebrews to Israelites and developed systems of law and monarchy and census and more. Leviticus, Numbers, and Deuteronomy are prequels to Exodus. All are birthed from this book and the story of how they build a nation of people.

Also known as the Torah, these first five books of the Hebrew Bible (the Pentateuch), are based on the stories of Abraham, Isaac, and Jacob, 400 years of slavery, and how Moses was used by God to deliver His people; the night of Passover is the night before they left. Many of the customs we see today come out of this one book of the Bible: Exodus. Jesus was Jewish. Jesus's brother, James, is the author of the book of James in the New Testament. It reads differently when you know that James was a devout Jew writing to other Jewish leaders—those who followed the Torah with zeal. You will read that book differently than the books written by Paul (who wrote to Gentiles) when you see the culture that James came from and the history of the people he is speaking to. There is so much about our spiritual culture that is based on these moments in Exodus. When we have this context, it changes the way we read and digest the Word of God.

God promised Abraham, Isaac, and Jacob that they would birth a nation of holy people and be as many as the sand and stars. But holding onto promises when times are hard is not as easy as it seems. It's not easy to hold onto hope and allow it to build your faith, but we are about to learn how the Israelites do exactly that.

Where Our Story Begins
READ GENESIS 50:24-26

> [24] "Then Joseph said to his brothers, 'I am about to die. But God will surely come to your aid and take you up out of this land to the land he promised on oath to Abraham, Isaac and Jacob.' [25] And Joseph made the Israelites swear an oath and said, 'God will surely come to your aid, and then you must carry my bones up from this place.' [26] So Joseph died at the age of a hundred and ten. And after they embalmed him, he was placed in a coffin in Egypt."

Joseph believed in the promise of God to his ancestors. He remembered that Abraham was to become the father of a nation, and although he would not live to see it, he knew he could hold onto hope that his bones would enter into the land of promise.

This is where our story begins. Abraham's descendants ended up in Egypt and (in part because of the testimony of Joseph) found favor with Pharaoh, receiving a blessing of the most fertile land in Egypt—Goshen.

They multiplied as promised, and before long they grew to a nation of over two million (we find this count during the census performed in Numbers). Moses arrived on the scene and as he led them out of slavery, their identity shifted from Hebrew to Israelite. They became their own nation, much like other nations at that time: Egyptians, Canaanites, Amalekites, Hittites, Babylonians, Assyrians, Arameans, Amorites, Perizzites, etc. From Hebrews to Israelites.

Mistreatment and Misidentification

The word *Hebrew* only occurs a couple of dozen times in the Old Testament and it usually is found in context and connected to an enslaved person. The word is often used in a dismissive, insulting way by Egyptians and Philistines. It appears to reflect not so much an ethnic group as a lower class of people.

READ GENESIS 43:32

> *"They served him by himself, the brothers by themselves, and the Egyptians who ate with him by themselves, because Egyptians could not eat with Hebrews, for that is detestable to Egyptians."*

Notice anything about the way Joseph was treated in comparison to the Egyptians? He was set aside—not included. Despite being in a position of authority, Joseph was still degraded and disrespected.

Hebrews were not yet known as "Israelites." They weren't even a nation yet. We know that they were set apart and God had great promises in store for them, but at that time they were slaves living in a foreign land. How often do we find ourselves living more like Hebrews than Israelites? Waiting on our promise, waiting on something to happen—doors shut, feeling dismissed, fighting to see if there is more out there in this big world called life for us?

Can you relate?

Maybe like the Hebrews, you have forgotten the promises before you.

Maybe you have a vague recollection of the inheritance of your lineage, or you are in a place right now that looks very different from the dreams you had as a child.

Life has happened, time has passed, and you wake up one morning and think, *Wasn't I supposed to be an Israelite? Why am I still a Hebrew?*

Exodus carries the promise to move these two million Hebrew descendants of Abraham, Isaac, and Jacob, out of slavery and oppression into their own land and establish themselves as a holy nation.

This is that story.

Without that rich history, albeit a very high level look chronologically, some may miss that this entire story is birthed out of a promise.

Look up the promises of God in these passages and make note of what was promised:

Gen. 1:28	_____
Gen. 9:1	_____
Gen. 12:1–20	_____
Gen. 17:2,6; 22:17	_____
Gen. 26:4; 28:14	_____
Gen. 35:11; 48:4	_____

A Prayer

God, thank You for the promises You've made to Your people. Thank You that You are a trusted promise keeper, and that You are going to keep Your word to me in the same way You've kept your word to Abraham and his descendants. Amen.

Questions for Reflection

» Write out any promises you remember from God over your life.

» What did you used to daydream about as a kid?

» Do you have any spiritual inhertance you want to acknowledge and start addressing?

» Do you see any connection between childhood dreams and the promise you're walking in now or waiting on?

» Have you ever felt dismissed in your life? What do you need to hear God say to you about that?

» Consider making a genogram—a spiritual family tree—and look into what you have inherited, good and bad, and pray over it either way.

Journal

Think about a time you had a promise develop differently than you imagined. How did it make you feel when you realized your plans or expectations were different from what God had in store? How did you respond? Journal for a few minutes in full honesty and let your own experience of being led by God come to life on these pages.

TUESDAY

Like Jacob, He's Changed Your Name

I followed the tour guide through the halls of the Capitol building, in awe of the works of art that filled the halls with beauty. Giant murals lined the walls, and I was fascinated by the stories of American history that each of them told. Around one corner I stopped and stared at a beautiful painting that sat on an easel. It depicted a woman in a long white dress standing on the steps of an altar. The tour guide said her name: Pocahontas. I gasped.

When I lived a life of crime pre-Jesus, I was given the street name *Poca* (short for Pocahontas). I was called Poca for years. As a matter of fact, in a life of crime no one should know your real name for obvious reasons. After I turned my life around, I remember a woman telling me how she saw me in the store and called me by my real name (Rebecca), but I never turned around to greet her. I hadn't been called by my real name for years.

I continued staring at the painting, thinking about my past life and the name I hadn't thought of in years. I listened as the tour guide talked about Pocahontas.

"Then Pocahontas was baptized," said the man. "She was given the Christian name Rebecca."

I was undone.

Right there in the front of that painting I began to weep. No one else knew why I was crying. No one else knew that my old name was Poca. No one knew that the Lord was giving me back the name I was meant for. I realized, looking at that painting, that often what God calls us out of, he calls us to.

The History and the Promise
READ GENESIS 47:1-11

Jacob and his sons are coming from Canaan to settle in the land of Goshen, as a result of the famine in the land. The Pharaoh told Joseph that any able-bodied men in the family of Jacob could be directed to tend to the Pharaoh's livestock.

By settling in some of the finest land in Egypt (thanks to the blessing from Pharaoh), Jacob was looking toward a promise that was made to his father's father, Abraham. Maybe this was the land God had promised to Abraham. Maybe here, the children of God would eventually become a nation.

At the time of the promise, it seemed impossible because he and his wife Sarah were old. But Abraham believed God's promise, and eventually Isaac (Jacob's father) was born. So, this promise of becoming a great nation was a promise that was passed down from father to son, and then to grandson. And what a promise! Can you imagine how Abraham felt when God told him to sacrifice Isaac on the altar? (If you're not familiar with this story, read Genesis 22.)

This is an important moment of development that I don't want you to miss as you too go after your promise. I picture the moment when God told Abraham to lay Isaac on the altar as a test to see if he would choose obedience or the promise (as he understood it.) Dr. Bill Creasy, on his podcast "Scripture Uncovered," describes the moment of Abraham's strong fatherly hands tightening around his son as he pinned him down. Take a minute to think about this, picture it, process it. The haunting fear in Isaac's eyes staring at his dad who is pinning him down. We can imagine his strained, tearful, angry voice, "Father what are you doing? Stop it . . . You're hurting me." Did Abraham look Isaac in the eyes as he raised his blade, or did he look away with tears? Isaac was grown; this had to be a physical struggle between two grown men. The heartbreak Isaac was feeling in that moment. If you have grown up in an abusive home, you know all too well this look and the fear that rocks you to your core.

This traumatic moment had to impact Abraham and Isaac's relationship because after Genesis 22, there is not one further documentation of Abraham and Isaac interacting or speaking to each other. Nothing.

As a matter of fact, in Genesis 24:1–6, Abraham calls for *his servant* to find Isaac a wife from his lineage, and he does not even talk to his son about it. The transaction goes totally through the servant. As the storyline continues into Genesis chapter 25, after Sarah dies, Abraham takes a new wife and has six more children. But have you ever noticed what happens in verse 5?

"Abraham left everything he owned to Isaac."

Abraham left *everything* to Isaac. Six additional children, plus Ishmael from Hagar. Eight children in total and he left it all to one? Did he feel remorse? Regret? Did he die feeling tension with the son of his promise? It is always valuable when we can relate Scripture to a circumstance or situation.

>> Strained relationships can be hard. Do you have a strained relationship in your own life?
>> Do you worship your purpose, your promise, and your calling more than obedience?
>> Are you willing to lay your promise down if God asked you to?
>> Has anything in your life become an altar above God?

This story can be a catalyst in our own lives as we take stock of relationships and expectations and learn to lean into obedience and trust in God.

When we think of Bible characters like Abraham, Sarah, and Isaac, we tend to picture people in a story from long ago whom we can't necessarily relate to. We sweep by the incredibly relatable traumatic moments of familial struggle and relationship tension. We forget how often we pass on to our children what has been modeled to us. Science has proven in the last few years that unresolved trauma can be passed on genetically in the same way we pass on our hair and eye color.

Wrestling Through Conflict

Regardless of a possible strain in the relationship between his father and grandfather, Jacob held on to the promise that God would make his family into a great nation. He believed that someday they would be more than they were, more than simple Hebrews. I can imagine our shepherd friends sitting around a fire at night, looking up at the stars, wondering what *more* looks like. Wondering if God has something special in store for them. Have you ever daydreamed about a promise? Have you ever thought about it and then decided it wasn't for you? Maybe you thought you were too poor, came from too small of a town, didn't have connections, didn't have the experience or the know-how?

Walking with a Limp into Maturity

In Genesis 32:22 we find Jacob still waiting on this promise of a nation—a people group and a land that they can call their own. And in his desire to understand, he wrestles with an angel; some translations say it is with God Himself. In his struggle he is renamed Israel, which means "to contend with God," and he comes out with a limp from his hip being put out of joint.

Wrestling, questioning, fighting your way out of hard seasons will cause your walk to look a little different, friend. This can be the maturing that happens when you've lived through hard seasons and learn that it comes with a cost. We all want to be mature— to be able to stand firm and lean on God and do all the things we are told—but those Scriptures can be fleeting if we don't put them into practice when hard seasons come.

Wrestling it out in prayer with God instead of walking away is what we're called to do. The hardships you have endured in your lifetime will challenge you and they will change you. Like Jacob, you may have a new maturity and wisdom, but you'll walk with a limp.

As you continue, consider your own macro-level journey. Do you see any moments in your history that call for talking to God and wrestling it out with him? *Why me? Why did that door shut? Why did that pivot in my promise occur?* Write down what you need to hear Him say to you if you don't "feel" like you are hearing Him. Remember, it's these moments that shape our destiny because they shift our eyes off bitterness and to Him, the author and finisher of our faith, instead.

A Prayer

God, thank You for being the Father of new beginnings. You have seen the beginnings, the endings, and the in-betweens of my story, and You still believe I am worthy of Your promises. You are renaming me on this journey toward my promised land, and I am grateful to stir my thoughts toward the memories of Your faithfulness. Guide my heart back toward Your words and the work of Your hands in my life. Let me remember the moments You have engaged my story and be encouraged! Amen.

Questions for Reflection

» Do you have strained relationships from past trauma?

» Have you ever parented out of regret and, if so, are there things you want to change so that you can stop the unhealthy trauma responses?

» Have you considered that there have been times when people, things, or promises have been put in a position above God?

» Are there things your heart is longing for in this season?

» Are there things you want to list that need some time in lament, wrestling with God over your why?

» Ask God in prayer if He has a new name for you in this season. Don't use logic. Pick the first name that popped in your head and then research what it means.

WEDNESDAY

Choose Courage Over Fear

Growing up in a small logging town in Oregon, I never could have pictured what it would be like to live in a big city like Las Vegas. But it was interesting how quickly I became accustomed to the lights and sounds of the city once I got there. I became someone who could navigate heavy traffic and expansive casinos like a Las Vegas native. I had been assimilated into the culture before I knew it.

When I think of Egypt at its peak, I often picture scenes from movies like *Gladiator* and *300*. I envision the giant pillars, carvings, systems, and structures that Egypt encapsulated. While that was part of the

Roman Empire, Rome invaded Egypt and much of their empire reflects this landscape.

The Rich Culture of Egypt

It was a flourishing culture with agriculture, artisans, buildings, and a robust writing and mathematical system. Even with this vibrant, colorful culture, we know that groups of people did not mix within social castes in antiquity.

Our study finds itself in the historical time period of 1500–1200 BC, when the Egyptian Empire was at its absolute peak. It dominated the ancient world, one of the most powerful and iconic civilizations in history. The pyramids were over a thousand years old before Moses even came on the scene.

Egyptians wore kohl-rimmed eyes—a combination of coal and animal fat that had been mixed together along with other makeup—not only for decoration and status, but to help protect their faces from the harsh climate conditions in Egypt (hot sun and lots of dust and sand when the wind picked up). Most women wore elaborate wigs both for fashion and to protect themselves from the blazing desert sun.

Their art was exquisite, and there were detailed meanings behind specific colors, gems, and stones. They were the mecca of their day, with the Nile River bringing a huge number of resources to the region. Due to the reliance on artistic culture, artisan cities were common areas in Egypt. Their customs are well depicted through their hieroglyphics and tablets, showing varying artisans: scribes, wine pressers, blanket weavers, musicians, bakers, potters, carpenters, fishers, hunters, embalmers, professional wailers (yep, you heard that right, for funerals), ropemakers, and those involved in different stages of agriculture.

Their ancient formal writing system was hieroglyphics and consisted of over 1,000 distinct characters as well as syllables, cursive fonts, and more. Few civilizations were as advanced as Egypt and fewer still can claim their original discoveries are in use today. Their extremely advanced mathematics system, combined with astronomy, created the framework for our measurement system of 365 days around the sun as well as 24 hours in a day. It is said that Nefertiti's tomb had a design so intricate, the sun shone through on both her birthday and coronation. Even when recreated recently, scientists could only get the sun to shine through on her birthday, but not both. Their remarkable geometric precision created the cubit (foundational for building the pyramids) as well as the first method of measuring and surveying land. This created the most advanced civil engineering process of canal systems to move water from the Nile to all neighboring fields and cities, allowing life to flourish. Their advanced language of 700–1,000 characters and cursive hieratic, and the invention of papyrus paper with ink allowed their scribes to create an administration structure like never before seen! Their culture spread quickly and flourished!

Enslavement in the Land of Goshen

More than 400 years after Jacob received his new name, the Hebrews find themselves in the land of Goshen on the outskirts of the thriving Egyptian metropolis. But they aren't really "neighbors." They have become slaves.

During the last 400 years, in the most fertile land of the Nile, Goshen, they had grown from 73 people to two million. Think about it, in this era, most girls were getting married and having children at sixteen or seventeen years old and on average had seven children. Run the numbers over 400 years and we actually see in Numbers that they are organized by tribe, counting 603,550 men of fighting age (20–50). Usually around 50 percent of a population is male and female so that would put the population at 1.2 million. Include anyone younger than twenty and over fifty, and we could easily count the population of Hebrews at two million.

Let's revisit the big picture. Abraham was promised that his descendants would be a nation. Isaac is born and later has Jacob. Isaac has trauma and Jacob wrestles through his trauma with God, receiving a new name: Israel. It is Jacob's sons that became *the* twelve tribes of Israel. This is the story of how the Hebrew people became the Israelites.

READ EXODUS 1:8-10

> [8] *"Then a new king, to whom Joseph meant nothing, came to power in Egypt.* [9] *'Look,' he said to his people, 'the Israelites have become far too numerous for us.* [10] *Come, we must deal shrewdly with them or they will become even more numerous and, if war breaks out, will join our enemies, fight against us and leave the country.'"*

We will get into which new Pharaoh of the eighteenth-century BC stepped on the scene later but first we need to camp here for a minute.

The favor that we all remember Joseph receiving in Genesis is gone. Now a new Pharaoh is anxious to rule with his own mind and desires. And he is not keen to start mixing the social castes, because the structure is what provided the stable authority for Pharaoh in the first place. Generally, in Egypt the varying social castes are categorized into three sections: royal, free, and slave.

Protecting the Lineage of Egypt

The Hebrews were living as slaves in Goshen. But why would the Egyptians want to make life miserable for the Jews? Israel was a source of blessing in the land, as Joseph had been before them (Gen. 39:1–6), and they weren't causing trouble. So, what reason could this Pharaoh have to remove the favor on Jacob and his people? For the answer, we can look to Exodus 1:10:

> *"Come, we must deal shrewdly with them or they will become even more numerous and, if war breaks out, will join our enemies and fight against us and leave the country."*

Fear. Pharaoh's stated reason was that the presence of so many Jews was a security risk. Since the Jews were outsiders—and mistreated ones at that—in the event of an invasion, they would no doubt ally themselves with the enemy. Goshen is along the international trade route of Via Maris that approaches from the north. Two million mistreated slaves would be the greeting party to any invaders, and Pharaoh knew this was a real concern for Egypt: Winning a war does not begin with an initial encounter between your enemy and the oppressed, enslaved people in your country.

History shows us there were three primary periods during ancient Egypt's lifespan known as the first, second, and third kingdoms. The time between these eras are known as Intermediate periods when Egypt was divided among itself due to rulership. The third period is known as the new kingdom, when Egypt finally reaches its peak and Moses steps onto the scene. The pharaohs during this third period are military driven. They do not want to end up like the first two kingdoms and so become more strategic and advanced in their tactics. They are unprecedented with their invasion tactics, so it makes sense why suddenly, the interest has shifted culturally to invasion and protection.

The name *Pharaoh* actually means "great house" and was a position believed to be passed through birth as god-like beings. His many wives not only assisted in ensuring that his legacy was established, but also helped in the afterlife and were used as a social contract with other countries.

Egyptian court in the eighteenth and nineteenth dynasties was known to employ large numbers of state slaves (hence the story of Joseph) as well as for building projects. Wars between Egypt, Asia, Syria, the Arameans, the Hittites, and the Canaanites had taken place, and boundary lines and treaties for trade were established.

Egyptian royal customs were specific, such as eating in order of birthright, but they also had very specific bathing customs, as cleanliness was to be kept up for the afterlife. This is opposite from many slaves and even the free caste in Egypt, where bathing was done in the Nile. The Pharaoh was the deity-like ruler who was equal to a god in their pantheon. A pantheon is a group of gods in a specific religion. A more known example is Greek mythology and gods and goddesses such as Zeus and Aphrodite. Egyptian religion had their own entire pantheon with stories of creation and what each god represented. The Pharaoh was believed to deliver the messages to the gods. He acted as a divine liaison between humanity and the hundreds of gods.

Egyptians were forced to work part-time as a method of taxation to build pyramids. However, as armies, store cities, and temples grew, they needed more manpower. The Hebrews were the perfect caste system to enslave to assist in this building frenzy.

Specifically, two new store cities were important to this strategic military push. Circle the names of the store cities mentioned in verse 11:

READ EXODUS 1:11-16

[11] *"So they put slave masters over them to oppress them with forced labor, and they built Pithom and Rameses as store cities for Pharaoh.* [12] *But the more they were oppressed, the more they multiplied and spread; so, the Egyptians came to dread the Israelites* [13] *and worked them ruthlessly.* [14] *They made their lives bitter with harsh labor in brick and mortar and with all kinds of work in the fields; in all their harsh labor the Egyptians worked them ruthlessly.*

[15] *The king of Egypt said to the Hebrew midwives, whose names were Shiphrah and Puah,* [16] *'When you are helping the Hebrew women during childbirth on the delivery stool, if you see that the baby is a boy, kill him; but if it is a girl, let her live.'"*

How does this Pharaoh solve the problem of the growing population and fear that the slaves will join their enemies if invaded? Boys grow up and become warriors. Girls grow up and become servants. And because this killing of males would force Hebrew girls to intermarry, soon the Hebrew genealogy would be no more.

READ EXODUS 1:17-22

> *17 "The midwives, however, feared God and did not do what the king of Egypt had told them to do; they let the boys live. 18 Then the king of Egypt summoned the midwives and asked them, 'Why have you done this? Why have you let the boys live?'*
>
> *19 "The midwives answered Pharaoh, 'Hebrew women are not like Egyptian women; they are vigorous and give birth before the midwives arrive.'*
>
> *20 "So God was kind to the midwives and the people increased and became even more numerous. 21 And because the midwives feared God, he gave them families of their own.*
>
> *22 "Then Pharaoh gave this order to **all** his people: 'Every Hebrew boy that is born you must throw into the Nile, but let every girl live.'" [emphasis added]*

The midwives describe the Hebrew women giving birth as vigorous. Sounds complementary, or almost brave, right? The words *vigorous* or *lively* or *strong* may sound strong and full of life, but the phrase here in Hebrew, *haye*, is actually derogatory. It could be better translated as "like barbarians" or "like animals." The midwives described these Hebrew mothers with disdain, disrespect, and disgust even though they were protecting them from Pharaoh's decree.

Choosing the Higher Way

Pharaoh failed to account for a group of God-fearing midwives who feared God more than they feared man. They were willing to face fear with courage and not give in to Pharaoh's decree, instead choosing obedience to God.

Have you ever felt the social pressure to do something you knew was wrong? Think about a time you felt like you chose integrity and righteousness over social pressure or maybe wrestled with God about times you may have fallen short.

Baby after baby was thrown into the river to drown, and the wails from the Hebrew mothers reached the heavens. The mighty Nile—the very thing that was lifegiving for this region—was used to take life away from these families. The seasonal waterway that brought prosperity to the Egyptians was used to bring a season of despair to the Hebrew slaves.

If you're anything like me, you may wonder why God has allowed His people to be oppressed. Why does He allow death? I have often cried out to God wondering the same thing about people I love and situations of evil all around us. I hate that evil entered this world, but I trust God will use any situation and bring some resolve, purpose, and strength through it.

A Prayer

God, Your plans are better than ours. Your ways are higher than our ways. Your thoughts are greater than our thoughts. Though we may find ourselves confused and facing an uncertain future, You are intending everything we encounter as a stepping-stone on the path to bring glory to Your name. Thank You for always listening to my cries for safety, security, and clarity. I trust that You are over all I will face. Amen.

Questions for Reflection

» Have you ever experienced a situation as desolate as the one Israel faced?

» Take a moment to write out a few things that you've seen that demonstrate how God hears your cries! Ask Him to show you where He was listening.

» Have you been in situations that end up forcing you out of a comfort zone?

» What oppressions have you endured in the last year or season of your life? Do you believe that God will come through for you just like He did for Israel? Why or why not?

» What are some ways you can hold to God's promises in the midst of really hard times?

THURSDAY

It All Revolves Around the Pantheon

I can remember the Vegas skyline like it was yesterday. Every time I think of it, I get a bit of a pit in my stomach. It's the bondage I remember. The familiar smell of a casino. The drunk men who gawk and make cat calls at any girl within eyeshot. The memories contort my face; my jaw gets a sick twinge in the back even as I write about it now. I can remember nights where I walked Ellis Boulevard looking for a phone and drugs with my baby wrapped in a blanket, thrown over my shoulder. I was stuck in my addiction with bondage so extreme I didn't even recognize my chains. I thought I was fine. We were fine. I'd figure it out. I'd make it happen. I'd turn a trick or catch a date and things would be fine. At least that's the denial I was living in.

That's the crazy thing about bondage: You don't realize you're trapped until you hit rock bottom. You justify and excuse or normalize all the behaviors. Even if it is not outright "bondage" that feels extreme, we all have habits, characteristics, and thought patterns that very well may have been mirrored for us as children, that we think are fine.

I want to take another look at Exodus 1:11. American author and theologian John N. Oswalt says it best:

> The plan was simple enough. They would enslave the Israelites, not merely limiting their freedom to develop military skills, but also limiting their power to pick up and move out. But there was a further intent, and that was to break their spirits or "wear them down." The very "anah" [TH6031] can be translated in several ways including "afflict" and "humble" but the underlying sense is "to put down." God had dramatically exalted the people and now the Egyptians were setting out to reverse that. They believed that a thoroughly subjugated people would lose the will to resist.

Isn't that how sin works? It weasels into our lives to burden, afflict, and wear us down until we would lose the will to resist.

Remaining Set Apart

We read earlier that the children of Israel had not assimilated into Egyptian culture. They lived in Goshen, working as slaves and free labor to build the pyramids. But they knew of God from their forefathers. They knew the fear of the Lord, which is why the midwives would not assist in the demands of Pharaoh. And how did God respond to their obedience?

READ EXODUS 1:20-21

> [20] *"So God was kind to the midwives and the number of people increased and became even more numerous. [21] And because the midwives feared God, he gave them families of their own."*

But that's not all! Pharaoh misunderstood the loyalty of the midwives to God, but he also failed to account for the fact that regardless of his influence or power, he was not going toe to toe with another human or even a demigod, but with the God of the universe who had committed long to elevating the descendants of Abraham into a great nation.

READ EXODUS 2:23-25 (ESV)

> [23] *"During those many days the king of Egypt died, and the people of Israel groaned because of their slavery and cried out for help. Their cry for rescue from slavery came up to God. [24] And God heard their groaning, and God remembered his covenant with Abraham, with Isaac, and with Jacob. [25] God saw the people of Israel—and God knew."*

There is nothing as crucial in Egyptian culture as their religion; it was completely integrated into every aspect of daily life. The Egyptian religion incorporated practices and beliefs that combined mythology, herbology, science, magic, spirituality, and psychiatry.

Temples were the center of economic and political life and of course religion in ancient Egypt. Temples were considered the home of the gods and goddesses that the priests and priestesses were assigned. They required immense care, accomplished through elaborate rituals. Every person participated in three daily prayers as a ritual of daily ceremony.

They included very specific steps: opening a door to awaken the god, washing the idol, and sweeping away any footprints to ward off evil from coming around it.

Economically, much like other professions, priests and priestesses were passed on hereditarily, including a high priest per god or goddess. Everyone tithed to the temple, and the educated class would divide up the goods equally which led to a lot of corruption where Pharaohs would offer higher positions if the temple priests would give them larger portions of land and surplus.

Festivals throughout the year were dedicated to worshiping and thanking gods which created a social climate for many Egyptians.

The Pantheon

More than anything the pantheon consisted of hundreds (if not thousands) of deities. Some were regional or over a city while others represented nature and events. Each family got to choose who and how they worshiped their specific gods, but all worshiped nine main gods that we'll explore more deeply in lesson 3. Regardless of what caste system you were born into, the afterlife was thought to be real. Egyptians believed that your social status would determine your burial ritual, but you couldn't escape the afterlife.

The main belief (regardless of class or location) was that out of a watery abyss, a mound appeared, and a lotus flower blossomed. From the lotus flower birthed Ra-Atum, later shortened to simply Ra, but seen in hieroglyphics interchangeably. Ra is the guide of Pharaoh and god of the sun. Shu, the god of air and wind, married Tefnut, the goddess of moisture; they had Geb and Nut, a husband and wife who are often shown together in hieroglyphs and represented earth and sky together.

They gave birth to four children: Set (god of chaos), Osiris (god of Egypt), Isis (goddess of motherhood and magic), and Nephthys (goddess of protecting families). The myth is that in a jealous rage, Set dismembered Osiris and his wife/sister Isis roamed the land collecting all his pieces, except his manhood that was eaten by a fish. Once she collected all his body, she and Nephthys joined forces, and put Osiris back together. His virality came back but only long enough to impregnate Isis and pass on his lineage before dying again. Anubis and Horus were born and became god of the afterworld because he set off to find Set and avenge his father's death.[2]

It was believed that whatever you did on earth was carried to the afterlife. When you passed away, your heart would be weighed and if it was heavier than a feather, it was believed to be full of sin and you were eaten by a god named Sebek in the afterlife. If it was lighter than the feather, your soul passed into the Field of Reeds where no harm or sadness resided. Here, you would be reanimated and continue to live in harmony doing the same profession as before. Mummification was an integral part of the afterlife, ensuring your heart and head were intact to assist in reanimating you; therefore, much care went into preservation of the body. Whatever you drew or wrote on your sarcophagus (the Egyptian's coffin that held persons who had gone through a very ritualistic mummification process), would follow you into the afterlife and by it you would be remembered. This is why Pharaoh and his wive's tombs were so important and why the Valley of Kings is still such an incredible landmark today.

A Culture of Myths

Among many other rituals and behaviors, religious seers would inscribe prayers on elephant tusks to ward off evil spirits in a nursery. Egyptians also believed that Ra the sun god died every night and passed through the afterlife—during that time Set could use his chaos for good, helping Ra to conquer the snake and reemerge each morning. The Apis Bull, a highly respected deity, was greatly revered. Even Alexander the Great paid respects to his temple when he visited Memphis.

Egyptologists spend their entire life's work understanding the intricate details of this culture, assisting universities and museums that feature Pharaohs, their queens, and their tombs. My brief study will not do the complexity and beauty of their culture the justice it deserves.

But I wanted to paint enough of a picture for you of the deep, rich, and structured religion of Egypt. Life in Egypt was nothing without their belief system.

What I love about investigating the surroundings of our story is that it allows us to picture daily life for our characters. I know it may seem like we are focusing a lot on the deities and pantheon of Egyptian culture, but again, context is crucial! We need to learn how to visualize these details in order to understand how significantly they will impact our characters as we journey through the rest of the book of Exodus. And in studying about their lives, we may even learn something about our own journeys.

A Prayer

God, thank You for calling us to put our dreams on the altar before You. You are worth the trouble and time it takes to look at our hearts and consider our motives. Give us mercy for ourselves as we become introspective and self-aware. Holy Spirit, reveal to us anything we've placed ahead of God in our lives. We want to lay down our idols and pursue that which brings true life to us and those around us. Amen.

Questions for Reflection

» Make some notes of promises God gives when we trust His plan and not our own:

» What are some of the promises God offers you when you trust His plan and not your own? Make a list; start with these Scriptures if you need a jumping-off point.
- o Romans 8: 28–30
- o Proverbs 3:5–6
- o Genesis 50:20

FRIDAY

The Nile: The Lifeline of Egypt
READ EXODUS 1:8–22

In southern Oregon, the Rogue River is the center of outdoor activity and tourism. People come from all over to float or fish, and there's even a jet boat race in the center of my hometown every year. Local farmers use the mighty Rogue to irrigate and water their crops, and the region flourishes because of the steady flow of life-giving water that faithfully makes its way to the Pacific Ocean. I am sure any of you who live near bodies of water can make a list of ways that your community relies on varying trades or resources that come from this fresh source.

On a grander scale, the Nile River was a lifeline to Egypt and was the center of this dazzling culture.

Because our story takes place in the land of Goshen, where Joseph's extended family was given the best land by Pharaoh, we must take some time to explore where Goshen was on the Nile Delta, the northeastern portion right on the Via Maris. Not only was this some of the most fertile land due to irrigation and location, but it was the hub of the trade route connecting King's Highway with the Via Maris.

"Via Maris is one modern name for an ancient trade route, dating from the early Bronze Age, linking Egypt with the northern empires of Syria, Anatolia, and Mesopotamia—along the Mediterranean coast of modern-day Egypt, Palestine, Israel, Iran, Iraq, Turkey, and Syria. It is a historic road that runs in part along the Israeli Mediterranean coast. It was the most important route from Egypt to Syria.

"One earlier name was 'Way of the Philistines,' a reference to a passageway through the Philistine Plain (which today consists of Israel's southern coastal plain and the Gaza Strip). Academic researchers prefer other names, for instance 'International Trunk Road' or 'International Coastal Highway.'

"Together with the King's Highway, the Via Maris was one of the major trade routes connecting Egypt and Mesopotamia. The Via Maris was crossed by other trading routes, so that one could travel from Africa to Europe or from Asia to Africa."[3]

Life on the Nile

The Nile is the longest river in the world. It has three unique predictable seasons that cities in ancient Egypt built and planned around all year. In contrast, the nations around them were at a constant battle for better conditions. Their water supplies were sporadic and had no predictable seasons, bringing floods out of nowhere and decimating their communities. This is one of the main reasons Egypt remained as one of the most stable nations for thousands of years. The goddess Ma'at, for example, was thought to represent harmony.

The Nile had three predictable seasons: Akhet (inundation), Peret (emergence), and Shemu (harvest). The Akhet season was typically flooding and created silt that was incredibly fertile and allowed a huge, lush agriculture area in the midst of the Arab desert.

Egyptian culture was so advanced mathematically that their measurement system created one of the most advanced irrigation canals that flowed throughout all the cities around the Nile. School was only for the wealthy upper class and most children adopted whatever their fathers taught them as their family trade. House of Life was what this elite school was referred to. It was reserved for Physicians, Scribes, Astronomers, Architects, Diplomats, and more. It would be considered similar to a Harvard or other Ivy League school today.

Hieroglyphics and cursive known as hieratic are still some of the most admired of all times. Their organized administration system, thriving scribe profession and invention of papyrus paper allowed their writing system to spread quickly.

Most inhabitants, albeit within a strong social caste system, were regular working-class people and had their own family specialty: fish, wheat, barley, figs, etc. Whatever your family did is what was passed onto you. The idea of money and coins was not yet introduced until the Roman Empire, so bartering and trading your goods was what everyone relied on. If your family—a husband and wife with two kids—were barley growers, then they typically had a small crop around their home, a silo to store it, cats to keep mice away, an ox to help with soil and threshing. And their lives revolved around the seasons of the Nile.

Since industrial mechanisms for plowing or fishing or creating pottery had yet to be invented, the Egyptians are known to have created a Shaduf and other special irrigation tools that ensured consistent access to canals. No crops meant no food and nothing to trade. All the family helped out during these three seasons a year. Life without the Nile was impossible.

During Aket, the flood season, one could expect to have their area inundated with silt, and this time was often spent repairing the canals that helped their livelihood. During Peret, it was time to sow seed, and Shemu was time to gather the crops and trade.

Ultimate Survival

The Nile was a true lifeline for everything else—bathing, using the restroom, etc. It was sickening to drink so most families drank wine, which is often depicted in hieroglyphics. Also since there was no freezing or refrigeration system, items spoiled easily and so milk and meat were very rare for the commoner in Egypt. Besides, most of their livestock was used to help toil land, thresh wheat, and pull hoes. What's more, the Nile was full of deadly crocodiles and hippos. Without quality medical care and hard labor mixed with harsh conditions, most people outside of the palace had a life expectancy of around 50–60 years old.

Cities flourished all along the shores of this lifegiving river: Heliopolis, Memphis, Abydos, Thebes, Nekhen, and more. This area was broken into two regions: Upper and Lower and went in accordance with the direction of the flow of the Nile, meaning that the upper Nile was actually further south and the lower region was in the north of Egypt where the Nile dumped into the Mediterranean Sea.

All up and down the Nile, we see the way the mighty river nourished the land and its people. We can imagine children growing up along its banks, learning to worship the gods to ensure the water will continue to flow. Children followed the footsteps of their parents, maintaining rituals, wealth, and crediting their flourishing land to their ability to continue pleasing the gods of the land and sky.

Holding Back Your Bitterness

Imagine you are a neighboring country to Egypt. It would be simple to assume the Egyptians were correct; things seemed easier for them because of the predictable nature of the Nile. Were they more blessed? It probably felt that way. Our Western church world can often seem this way as well. If we are the people with the most money, access, followers, contracts, homes, cars, etc., then we MUST have the favor of God in our lives and decisions, right? That attitude will destroy our hope and promise faster than locusts destroying the crops.

If we keep the perspective that someone's outside wealth or status equates to the favor of God, we are on a fast track to disappointment, envy, covetousness, and pride. We have to check those thoughts before they take root in our hearts.

If we saw outward success as the only sign of favor in someone's life, then we would completely miss the stories about Job and Jesus Himself!

The Bible says it rains on the just and the unjust alike. Working to obtain God's blessing is the last thing He wants. He desires the investment of our hearts; otherwise we'd obey His laws to create an exchange, not to enter into a true relationship. He wants family, not robots.

What counts as success? James 4:17 states, "If anyone, then, knows the good they ought to do and doesn't do it, it is sin for them." Success can be defined as achieving objectives or personal fulfillment. We know as believers that this depends greatly on our faithfulness to God, to do what we know we ought to do. Success without that can lead to dependence on one's own strength instead of God.

JOSHUA 1:7 STATES:

"Only be strong and very courageous, being careful to do according to all the law that Moses my servant commanded you. Do not turn from it to the right hand or to the left, that you may have good success wherever you go." (ESV)

What is so fitting about this verse is that this command is in direct response to the children of Israel taking over their promised land, but it takes courage and maybe from places least expected.

A Prayer

God, I confess I have felt the unfair nature of financial and physical gifts in this life. I have harbored resentment, bitterness, and jealousy at the advancement of others. I have grown weary, waiting for my promise and rejected the truth of a life spent trusting and focusing on You. You have a better method and plan for my story than I can even imagine; bring my heart and intention back to Your Word and Your call for my life. Show me how You are using my story, even now, while I am waiting for the promise to be fulfilled. Show me when to step in courageously to the arenas You are calling me to step into. Amen.

Questions for Reflection

» What similarities between Egyptian culture and your own do you see today?

» Have you ever considered your background, your family line, your city, and thought, *"God can never use me . . ."*? If yes, write that lie down here.

Then cross it out and write the word "LIE" next to it. Good therapy.

» Have you ever assumed that someone received a greater measure of favor than you because of the physical "fruit" or "blessing" you saw in their lives? How did that comparison effect your ability to receive your own measure of "fruit" or "blessing"?

» Read Matthew 5:45: It rains on the _____ and the _____ alike. Wrestle with God around how that makes you feel.

» What is God asking you to step into courageously in this season?

REMEMBER WHO YOU ARE

THE SUN WAS STRONG as Moses sat leaning against a rock with just enough shade for everything except his feet. He scratched his beard and watched the animals find what little grazing was available amid the rough terrain. He leaned his head back and sighed deeply. The sweat and sticky air mixed with the dust leaving dirt creases on his neck. He closed his eyes and remembered his childhood, playing near the Nile River with other kids from the palace. Chasing cats and netting fish. The women were always so well dressed and immaculate. Clean. Moses smiled, remembering the bathing routines they followed daily. *Shave your head to keep lice away, scrub your body with the soda ash and oil, splash on perfume, grab a mint leaf for your breath.* He laughed, thinking, "If the princess could see me now." His mind drifted to his adopted mother. She loved him dearly. He knew he was different; his sister and real mom had told him. He was special—that's what they said. He had been saved from death when others had not. But he had few memories of his real mom now. He was so little when he was sent to the Pharaoh's house. But the princess was a courageous and loving woman to him. She'd always ask about his writing and astrology after school, making sure the kids were being nice to him.

His mind drifted to the House of Life, the temple school for Pharaoh's house and other wealthy families The first day he arrived at school, he walked slowly in awe, gripping his satchel draped over his chest. He looked up at the giant pillars and colorful hieroglyphics that seemed to touch the sky. *This must be what the Field of Reeds, the afterlife, looks like.* His teachers were patient but firm, ensuring he worked on learning to read and write. He knew learning here was a privilege. He remembered from his street friends that they couldn't afford to attend. They had to fill the roles of their fathers, inheriting the family trade: baker, embalmer, fisherman. He smiled, remembering copying down the chants from the Book of Spells and selling them with the other kids in the court to earn money for the temple. He laughed, shaking his head. What a life.

Moses opened his eyes, sitting up to look at the flock of sheep still meandering for food. The sun had crept up exposing his shins and knees as well. He dropped his head and drew a hieroglyphic symbol in the dirt. His remembrance turned to regret.

How did I get here? What have I done? I was supposed to be a diplomat, a professor. These aren't even my sheep—they're Jethro's! Why couldn't I have just bit my tongue and kept my mouth shut? Oh, I am grateful for the people in my life, but this isn't how I expected my life to turn out . . .

JUST AROUND THE CORNER

When we think of Moses, I am guessing that most of us imagine a bearded man in his old age, leaning on his staff and insisting with a loud, stuttering voice to Pharaoh that he should let his people go. If you attended Sunday school as a child, you may be able to close your eyes and see the flannel board as Moses takes his famous journey out of Egypt with sheep, camels, and his flock of hopeful followers. However, we'd be remiss to not take a moment to remember the first half of Moses's life, the years when he was still a young family man, full of regrets and dreams about what should have been.

Or we can go even further back to when he was a baby, gently lowered into a river basket, his mother's hands shaking as she kissed him good-bye, pushing him down shore toward the reeds where the princess was bathing. I picture his big sister hiding in the tall reeds, carefully wading through the water, heart pounding, praying with all her might for her baby brother. Oh, how Miriam must have raced home to her mother after the princess's servants carried Moses to the palace. How she must have clutched her mother in excitement and grief, tears of relief falling as she explained their plan had worked. A desperate and beautiful act by two women, risking everything for this child who had come into the world in amid bloodshed and despair—a wild and brave hope fueled by a mother's love.

The Bible tells us that Moses was raised in Pharaoh's palace with all the nepotism and the privilege of those who are closely related to the king. Remember, Moses is brought up in an era where the Egyptian Empire is at its peak. He is given the best schooling in mathematics, writing, geometry, and reading, likely learning cursive hieroglyphs on papyrus paper. He is learning about the political structure of the Egyptian Empire and growing up worshiping the pantheon gods of Egyptian culture.

This is a culture obsessed with cats, the afterlife, and the worship of Ra among other gods and goddesses. We can imagine and deduct from what we just discovered of Egyptian culture and Scripture that Moses was on track to become a diplomat in Pharaoh's courts. His schooling, we know, is at the top of its time, very much like an Ivy League graduate would be today. He was supposed to do something great with his life. Although he knew the humble background of his birth mother, he was likely the first Hebrew to have an opportunity like this.

Maybe you can relate with Moses. Maybe you've had moments in your own life when you felt like a bad decision has altered your course. Maybe there's been something you've said or done that slammed an important door. Maybe you're dealing with the consequences of some actions or some choices that have destroyed your hopes and ruined your plans. Maybe a job loss or loss of another kind has caused you to question what you ever did with your degree or what's next in this season.

I want to encourage you that God is not done with you yet. He has a plan, a purpose, and a once-in-a-lifetime opportunity that doesn't go away or expire. Even in our setbacks he will continue to make a way for us. Who knows what would have happened if Moses had not murdered the soldier? It's not for us to know. Sometimes the way God gets our attention is different because of our choices, but the plan and the call on your life does not change. God doesn't change his mind and he doesn't make mistakes.

And besides, your burning bush may be just around the corner.

MONDAY

Providential Courage
READ EXODUS 2:1-10

---

[1] *"Now a man of the tribe of Levi married a Levite woman,* [2] *and she became pregnant and gave birth to a son. When she saw that he was a fine child, she hid him for three months.* [3] *But when she could hide him no longer, she got a papyrus basket for him and coated it with tar and pitch. Then she placed the child in it and put it among the reeds along the bank of the Nile.* [4] *His sister stood at a distance to see what would happen to him.*

[5] *"Then Pharaoh's daughter went down to the Nile to bathe, and her attendants were walking along the riverbank. She saw the basket among the reeds and sent her female slave to get it.* [6] *She opened it and saw the baby. He was crying, and she felt sorry for him. 'This is one of the Hebrew babies,' she said."*

[7] *"Then his sister asked Pharaoh's daughter, 'Shall I go and get one of the Hebrew women to nurse the baby for you?'*

[8] *"'Yes, go,' she answered. So the girl went and got the baby's mother.* [9] *Pharaoh's daughter said to her, 'Take this baby and nurse him for me, and I will pay you.' So the woman took the baby and nursed him.* [10] *When the child grew older, she took him to Pharaoh's daughter and he became her son. She named him Moses, saying, 'I drew him out of the water.'"*

We begin Exodus chapter 2 with the recent decree that all the Hebrew baby boys are to be killed. This is when our star character comes on the scene. He is given the Egyptian name *Moses*, which means "to be drawn out." What's fascinating is that the meaning behind Moses's name is exactly what *he* ends up doing for his people. What we're called out of is often what we're called to.

Hebrew midwives were more afraid of God than they were of the edict of man, so they did not kill the Hebrew babies. It took their courage in the midst of fear of man's edict to stand up and do what God wanted them to do. The mother and sister of Moses also bravely intervened to save his life, intentionally putting him in a position to be noticed by another woman—the daughter of Pharaoh.

Out of the Water

Scripture tells us that Moses's mother described him as "fine" or "good," which is the same word in Hebrew that God used to describe creation when he was done in Genesis. It wasn't defined as "good manners," as we take that to mean in Western culture; it can be more adequately defined as something special. Moses was being literally pulled out of the water and set apart—this was the beginning of the promise for his life! This "something special" of God's influence on the life of Moses captured the attention of royalty. The favor of God, made manifest in the middle of an almost certain demise, led to Moses being raised in the palace of Pharaoh by yet another woman who also dismissed the decree of man to follow the cry of her heart.

It's important to REMEMBER these moments because they are the promises that God is not done with you! He has not forgotten you even when things seem bleak, unfair, or unfavored. THIS is when God does His BEST work.

Life in the Palace

Moses is raised and trained with the oppressors' resources and in the caste system we learned about in lesson 1. Let's cross reference what we are learning in Exodus with Acts chapter 7, where we learn more about Moses's upbringing while in Pharaoh's court.

TURN TO ACTS 7:17-22

[17] *"As the time drew near for God to fulfill his promise to Abraham, the number of our people in Egypt had greatly increased.* [18] *Then 'a new king, to whom Joseph meant nothing, came to power in Egypt.'* [19] *He dealt treacherously with our people and oppressed our ancestors by forcing them to throw out their newborn babies so that they would die.*

[20] *"At that time Moses was born, and he was no ordinary child. For three months he was cared for by his family.* [21] *When he was placed outside, Pharaoh's daughter took him and brought him up as her own son.* [22] *Moses was educated in all the wisdom of the Egyptians and was powerful in speech and action."*

Finding Providential Courage

When we look at the definition of each of the above words and combine them, you get:

The ability to do something that frightens one; strength in the face of pain, grief, or fear, occurring at a favorable time; opportune and involving divine foresight or intervention.

How many times have you chosen courage over fear in your life? I started using that feeling of fear as a barometer or guide on which direction I should be heading, not the path I should avoid. We can do this because we know that fear is not from God. We need to flip fear on its head! Ask yourself: *What is the enemy trying so hard to stop you from accessing?* Look fear in the face and step into the water, friend. He's got you!

A Prayer

God, I have faced trials I never expected in this life. The lows have been lower and the highs just as high, but still, You are faithful through each of the waves. Forgive me for losing sight of Your promises in the midst of unexpected defeat. Remind me of Your promises for courage, equipping, and clarity. Thank You for keeping me aligned with Your heart, and protecting me beneath Your wings. Amen.

Questions for Reflection

» Have you ever had a time when your situation seemed bleak, but God stepped in much like he did for Moses even as an infant?

» Do you see where God was for you in those moments of crisis?

» What does "providential courage" mean to you and for your story?

TUESDAY

He Has Not Forgotten About You
READ EXODUS 2:11-3:1

I had done it again. Put my foot in my mouth. And not just a slip of the tongue, said the "wrong thing" type of moment. This was a full-on flip out, directed at a pastor's wife whom I didn't even know. Yep. Guilty. I was embarrassed, and although I tried to apologize, she wasn't having it.

I wish I could tell you why. I bear good fruit; I know I do! I cried to a mentor who gave me a word that made me laugh: "Girl, you are Gordon Ramsey. Be a Gordon Ramsey! Do you know why he can do that? Because he's got the credentials to back it up and so do you!" I know my Spirit-filled friend wasn't inviting me to cuss out the people on my teams like *Hell's Kitchen*, but that he was calling me into forgiving myself.

Was I right in what I said? Absolutely. Did I deliver it with kindness and grace? Not at all.

Maybe you've never been there, sweet friend, and oh, bless your heart if you have never had one of those table-flipping moments in your life. But for me, this has happened more lately than I'd like to admit.

Then there were all of my excuses: burnout, triggered . . . and while everyone was focusing on me flipping over the table, I wanted to scream for them to see the root of the problem that preceded my explosion—the "corruption in the temple," if you will. It was like it all came pouring out and I couldn't stop the words from flying out of my mouth. The more I tried to justify my reaction, the deeper the hole beneath me became.

It was bad, girl. Bad.

As we read this next part of Scripture, I picture Moses doing the same thing.

READ EXODUS 2:11-15

> *¹¹ "One day, after Moses had grown up, he went out to where his own people were and watched them at their hard labor. He saw an Egyptian beating a Hebrew, one of his own people. ¹² Looking this way and that and seeing no one, he killed the Egyptian and hid him in the sand. ¹³ The next day he went out and saw two Hebrews fighting. He asked the one in the wrong, 'Why are you hitting your fellow Hebrew?'*
>
> *¹⁴ "The man said, 'Who made you ruler and judge over us? Are you thinking of killing me as you killed the Egyptian?' Then Moses was afraid and thought, 'What I did must have become known.'"*
>
> *¹⁵ "When Pharaoh heard of this, he tried to kill Moses, but Moses fled from Pharaoh and went to live in Midian, where he sat down by a well."*

The Fallout of Table Flipping

Imagine it: Moses is walking through the tight quarters of Rameses, kids running by, fathers plowing their plots of land. Suddenly, Moses catches sight of an Egyptian man beating a Hebrew, one of his people. Have you ever seen something so unjust it makes your blood boil? In Moses's rage, he flips out. He hopes his violence will go unnoticed, but clearly, someone saw him! Word has spread!

So, to avoid Pharaoh's capital punishment, he flees to Midian. Once there, he sat down by the well and surely was hit with guilt, shame, and regret. He severed opportunities and cut off relationships. He must have felt every possible emotion. As he sat there at the well, I wonder if he beat himself up mentally as much as I have (maybe as much as you have)? Did he have an inner critic like mine?

Sometimes our gifts become our weaknesses if we lack the maturity to manage them. That table-flipping story I mentioned? That happened a few months ago, at the same time I was writing this book, girl. This wasn't an old lesson I'd learned, no ma'am. It's a lesson I am still walking in. I am still learning how to quiet the rage I feel against the injustice I

49

see happening to the women I serve. No question, God is still working this out in me.

Let's keep reading.

READ EXODUS 2:16-22 (ESV)

> [16] *"Now the priest of Midian had seven daughters, and they came and drew water and filled the troughs to water their father's flock.* [17] *The shepherds came and drove them away, but Moses stood up and saved them, and watered their flock.* [18] *When they came home to their father Reuel, he said, 'How is it that you have come home so soon today?'* [19] *They said, 'An Egyptian delivered us out of the hand of the shepherds and even drew water for us and watered the flock.'* [20] *He said to his daughters, 'Then where is he? Why have you left the man? Call him, that he may eat bread.'* [21] *And Moses was content to dwell with the man, and he gave Moses his daughter Zipporah.* [22] *She gave birth to a son, and he called his name Gershom, for he said, 'I have been a sojourner in a foreign land.'"*

As Moses is sitting by the well in Midian, avoiding the consequences of his actions, young women approach to feed their flock. Some shepherds there began giving the women a hard time and Moses once again uses his heart for injustice and chases the shepherds off. The girls return home where their father Jethro insists that Moses stay with him. But look how they refer to Moses, "an Egyptian delivered us . . ." They didn't see Moses as a Hebrew; they saw his shaved head, his kohl-rimmed eyes, his clean face, and perfume scent. He was not a shepherd.

Moses becomes a member of Jethro's house. There he learned Hebrew customs. He tended to the flocks and learned about being a shepherd. It was tough work, much tougher than life at the palace. I picture how Moses must have felt, going from school to tending sheep. He probably missed his diet of fish and fruit.

READ EXODUS 3:1 (ESV)

> *"Now Moses was keeping the flock of his father-in-law, Jethro, the priest of Midian, and he led his flock to the west side of the wilderness and came to Horeb, the mountain of God."*

Forty years passed and we find Moses still tending to Jethro's flock, the scene we painted in the opening chapter. He didn't even have a flock of his own. We can only imagine that Moses was feeling defeated. We can only imagine that he was sitting there thinking things that we all may have thought such as, *What have I done with my life? I was supposed to be someone important. Why couldn't I have just bitten my tongue? Why do I always sabotage myself?*

Returning Home, Shame Free

I can relate to the story of the prodigal son (Luke 15:11–32). But the older I get (at my ripe age of 40, which feels much more like 25 most days), I realize that there was so much more to this rich story in the Gospels. Maybe unlike me, you have never really related to the prodigal son—running away from his dad to squander all his inheritance and end up in a heaping pile of mess. I would like to turn your attention to the older brother then. He stayed in his father's house and was still full of bitterness, envy, and anger. No matter which brother you identify with, we've all had times when the worst parts of ourselves have gotten the better of us and we find ourselves sitting beside a metaphorical well, on the run from our own behaviors wondering, *What have I done?*

Do you know what I love about God though? He knows exactly how your brain works. He knows the spiritual lineage (good and bad) that you have inherited. He knows the culture and community in which you were raised. He knows any of your past traumas or abuse. He knows your upbringing and your childhood. He knows the hard seasons you've

51

walked through and the walls that have built around your heart because of them. He knows the brokenhearted nights when your tears were collected in a bottle. He created your personality and your giftset, and He understands better than you the neurology and psychology you're working with. He knows how spiritual warfare will often put that nail strip in front of your speeding car to use your strength as a weakness, and guess what?

He still wants to use you. He still has plans for you. He still has promises and surprises that He wants to fulfill in your life.

A Prayer

God, You are the sole witness to every table I've ever flipped. Where I think I've hidden my shameful thoughts and behaviors, You witness and hold my heart close. Thank You for guiding me through the trials and traumas of my life. Remind me of Your faithfulness when all I feel is alone. Bring me closer to Your heart as I consider the reality of my tears and wonders of a future held in Your hands. Amen.

Questions for Reflection

» Think of Moses sitting by the well. Have you ever had a promise not turn out as expected?

» Can you think of a time in your life when a change of events made you wonder what in the world God was doing?

» Have you had a time when your behavior or action shut a door in your life? How did you take responsibility and repent?

» How can you allow God to change parts of your character that don't yet reflect the fruit of the Spirit?

WEDNESDAY

READ EXODUS 3:1-10 (ESV)

> ³ "Now Moses was keeping the flock of his father-in-law, Jethro, the priest of Midian, and he led his flock to the west side of the wilderness and came to Horeb, the mountain of God. ² And the angel of the Lord appeared to him in a flame of fire out of the midst of a bush. He looked, and behold, the bush was burning, yet it was not consumed. ³ And Moses said, 'I will turn aside to see this great sight, why the bush is not burned.' ⁴ When the Lord saw that he turned aside to see, God called to him out of the bush, 'Moses, Moses!' And he said, 'Here I am.' ⁵ Then he said, 'Do not come near; take your sandals off your feet, for the place on which you are standing is holy ground.' ⁶ And he said, 'I am the God of your father, the God of Abraham, the God of Isaac, and the God of Jacob.' And Moses hid his face, for he was afraid to look at God."
>
> ⁷ "Then the Lord said, 'I have surely seen the affliction of my people who are

in Egypt and have heard their cry because of their taskmasters. I know their sufferings, [8] and I have come down to deliver them out of the hand of the Egyptians and to bring them up out of that land to a good and broad land, a land flowing with milk and honey, to the place of the Canaanites, the Hittites, the Amorites, the Perizzites, the Hivites, and the Jebusites. [9] And now, behold, the cry of the people of Israel has come to me, and I have also seen the oppression with which the Egyptians oppress them. [10] Come, I will send you to Pharaoh that you may bring my people, the children of Israel, out of Egypt.'"

The Call Requires a Heart of Intensity

A while back, right after the birth of our third child, I started my own business. I ran it successfully for two years when I started to feel the tug on my heart to go into full-time ministry. I prayed and told the Lord that if He wanted me to do that, He was going to have to sell my business. I put it up for sale and it sold right away! But on the day of signing our contractual agreement, the buyers pulled out. I was crushed.

> ## "AN INTENSITY OF HEART IS WHAT WILL PUSH YOU THROUGH TO SEEK GOD IN THE DRIEST, MOST MUNDANE OF TIMES."
> ### —Art Katz

I had already started writing my first book and reaching out to groups and conferences to begin speaking. Here I was with a dream and suddenly a balloon popped. I won't lie; I was mad at God. I kept asking Him, *What kind of father would do that to their child: get their hopes up and then rip them away?* I heard no response but felt the presence of a dad holding a brokenhearted girl. I cried for several days, picturing a shiny red bike under the Christmas tree that was given away. A couple months later, I got another offer, and the sale of my business went through for exactly the amount I owed on it and not a dollar more.

I set out for ministry, but my faith had taken a real hit. I started self-doubting: doubting my ability to hear His direction, doubting my calling, doubting His goodness. How do I know if I step out in faith again that I won't be brokenhearted? What if I get disappointed again? Can I really trust Him to be a good God and a provider?

The Call to Action

Maybe I am not the only one who has experienced God saying, "not yet," "not this way," "keep waiting."

It was during this same doubting season that God called an adopted boy (now man) named Moses to action. God gave Moses direction for his calling while leading him along the backside, not the front, of Mount Horeb, by speaking to him through a burning bush. This is a miracle!

Horeb means "desolate," and a bush is the most ordinary of all scenery.[1] Have you had times of desolation—misery, unhappiness, a bleak outlook—from your past that God is calling you through? Have you ever felt too mundane or "normal" to accomplish any great feat? Well, perhaps you can take comfort in being in good company, because that is exactly how Moses felt, too. But God is not limited by your feelings or concerns about your calling. He doesn't call the wrong people! Regardless of what you have been through, or where you come from, if you have the tenacity and drive to chase after your destiny, nothing and no one can stop you because it is the Great I Am leading the way.

Maybe you don't feel the intensity of heart yet. Maybe you feel much like Moses did. What does Moses say to the Lord?

Ex. 3:11-12 _____

Ex. 4:1 _____

Ex. 4:10 _____

Ex. 4:13 _____

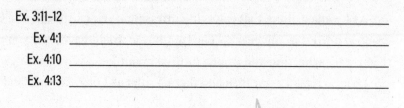

How did God respond to Moses's self-doubt? By affirming that not only was Moses the chosen one, but that God already foresaw his lack of confidence. He had planned on sending Aaron to Moses as a partner in this call. Despite feeling ill-equipped, God was prepared to both equip and provide Moses with a familiar partner, one with skills that Moses lacked. Moses did not believe he was ready for much of anything, let alone lead the Hebrews from captivity. God is not limited by our limitations, nor is he impressed by the humility that says, "We are not worthy of the call He has given us." He knows us, inside and out, just as he knew Moses. When the call of God comes into our lives, we can trust it is God's intention to be the driving force behind our purpose—because it is ultimately for His glory, not ours.

Equipped and Covered

Have you ever struggled with self-doubt? Maybe you thought God called you to something, but then it didn't come to pass? Possibly you feel inadequate or ill-equipped. What do you feel He is saying to you right now after learning more about how the great leader Moses began his journey?

A few years after my business sold, I finally got what I felt like was an answer from the Lord. Our state had passed a law that no longer allowed our type of business to be in existence. We had run an elective ultrasound center, doing gender-reveal parties for expecting mamas. The new law stated that medical devices could only be used for medical diagnostics. This actually shut down the business of the young woman who had successfully run the business after me. I was crushed for her and visited, asking if there was anything I could do to help. She was a woman of God and responded with grace and kindness, reminding me that I was not a fortune teller who could have seen these looming years ahead.

As I walked out of that emptying ultrasound center, the spirit of God dropped a word in my heart: "The first buyer would have sued you over this. I was protecting you from a future lawsuit."

I had to repent right then and there. I wept as I drove home. God had been protecting me and I didn't see it. I told God I was sorry for holding a grudge against Him, for letting bitterness seep into our relationship. My faith had taken a hit, but you know what? It takes a storm in our boat to increase our faith, doesn't it? My faith grew that day and, yes, it took a couple years, but it showed me that I have a good Abba, a loving Father who knows and sees the future, and I can trust Him even when I don't understand. Maybe you need to be reminded of the same.

READ ISAIAH 55:8-9 (KJV)

> [8] *"For My thoughts are not your thoughts, neither are your ways My ways,"* declares the Lord. [9] *"For as the heavens are higher than the earth, so are My ways higher than your ways and My thoughts than your thoughts."*

A Prayer

God, I confess I have spent many hours questioning the call on my life. I have questioned the timing and purpose of my actions and decisions. You have shown up on my behalf in ways I cannot comprehend, and I am ready for a deeper revelation of who You are in the middle of my messes. Holy Spirit, show me the places you have equipped me for my calling, covering me through the risks and preparing me to walk into this promise with confidence. Amen.

Questions for Reflection

» Have you had a time in your life when you felt like God abandoned His promise, or maybe you didn't hear Him correctly? Those trials definitely put a ding in our armor.

» Is there a time when your faith took a big hit like mine?

» Did you question the call on your life?

» How has any doubt derailed or distracted you from living the call on your life?

READ ROMANS 8:31

"If God is for us, who can be against us?"

» How does the declaration of God on your side change your perspective about the call on your life?

» What excuses can be dismantled in the presence of God's promises for your story?

THURSDAY

Human Agency
READ EXODUS 4:1-9

Admit it: We all become highly skeptical in the face of extravagant requests. Imagine if someone offered you a check for $100,000 to start the business of your dreams. This business will radically change your family, your community, and your entire life. They want no return on their investment. It's a gift, intended for you to use well and to enter into the future you've always hoped for—one of provision, work, intention, and contentment. I would be off the charts with skepticism, fear of future manipulation, and all kinds of other concerns. That level of call and generosity is hard to embrace. *What if I fail? What if I can't perform as I need to in order to honor this huge opportunity? What if I make too many mistakes and can't keep the work going?*

This is the same level of panic we hear from Moses, but God does not allow him to remain skeptical or afraid. He invites Moses to participate in miracles to demonstrate His dedication to Moses and freeing the Hebrews. Through each of the demonstrations, Moses faces his fears and seeks the Lord, using his will and human agency to partner with God in the call on his life.

Let's quickly recap the miracles that God had Moses perform for himself, the leaders, and Pharaoh in chapter 4:1–9:

1. God instructed Moses to throw his shepherd's staff onto the ground, turning it into a snake. When he retrieved the snake, it returned to the form of a staff.
2. God instructed Moses to tuck his hand into the fold of his cloak. Upon removal, the skin of his hand was white as snow with leprosy. He repeated the action and his hand was restored.
3. God instructed Moses to gather water from the Nile and pour it onto the dry ground, asserting that as the water was poured, it would become blood on the soil.

Remember, God doesn't need Moses to execute the plagues. He's simply the messenger. But with these three miracles, God is showing Moses that his involvement is crucial beyond that of being the heavenly mouthpiece. Moses has an opportunity to demonstrate the power and authority of God through each one. And they would have served as a warning and promise to Egyptians and Hebrews alike that God is not messing around. He is true to His word and will use any and everything to demonstrate His faithfulness to the promises He makes.

READ EXODUS 4:28-31 (ESV)

[28] "And Moses told Aaron all the words of the Lord with which he had sent him to speak, and all the signs that he had commanded him to do. [29] Then Moses and Aaron went and gathered together all the elders of the people of Israel. [30] Aaron spoke all the words that the Lord had spoken to Moses and did the signs in the sight of the people. [31] And the people believed; and when they heard that the Lord had visited the people of Israel and that he had seen their affliction, they bowed their heads and worshiped."

Moses had to partner with God in performing miracles. He had to step out and take a chance by going to the leaders forty years after running from Pharaoh's court. This takes a lot of trust in God, courage, and a yearning in your heart that you ARE intended to do great things.

Radical Changes

Moses faced so many limitations in his decision to partner with God. He resisted left and right, asking for a replacement. He traveled back to Egypt, meeting with Aaron in the wilderness. He had to recount all God had told him—with a straight face! From what we know of Moses, we can believe that he believed very little good about himself. His past told him he was a murderer, an outcast, and an orphan.

He lived in borrowed homes for his entire life, serving visions and households on behalf of someone else. His humility was not of God but from a false understanding of his identity in God. This was a man named for his being rescued from the waters. Before God would use him to rescue the Hebrews from slavery, Moses would need to start believing in his own ability to affect change and speak with confidence.

From the beginning, Moses was set apart. He lived among the Egyptians as a foreigner, adopted and given all the best things in life. But even throughout the events of his life, Moses never quite fit the mold of his own expectations. He needed an external reminder of his internal truth: that he was a child of the God of Abraham, Isaac, and Jacob. And he was meant to lead a life destined for the history books.

A Prayer

God, You see my weaknesses, faults, and fears. You hold my tears in Your hand, and You have never lost sight of who I am. Even when I am distracted, overwhelmed, and lost, You see my limitations. You send others alongside me to strengthen my heart and resolve. You offer Your own hand in partnership for my benefit and to Your glory. Thank You for leading me into the truth of Your promise for my life, and that You will not abandon me for making mistakes. Remind me who I am; remind me that I belong to You. Amen.

Questions for Reflection

» What radical life changes are needed for you to lean into the call on your life?

» How does the agency and engagement of Moses change the way you see your call?

» Has God asked you to partner with Him as a human agent to do something out of your comfort zone? What was the last thing He asked you to do that you haven't done yet?

» Are you witnessing the miracles of God manifest in your life in a way that provides confirmation of your call?

» Who does God say you are?

FRIDAY

It's Never Too Late
READ EXODUS 5:1

Out of all the Psalms that exist, only one is attributed to Moses: Psalm 90. Scholars assume Moses wrote this during his time with the Israelites, but it shows us his idea of life expectancy. Mark it in your Bible and read the words from our friend, his heart still burdened.

"90:10. life expectancy. Joseph died at the age of 110, considered the ideal age for an Egyptian. Examination of mummies has demonstrated that the average life expectancy in Egypt was between 40 and 50. The Egyptian *Papyrus Insinger* details those 10 years are spent in childhood and 10 more learning a trade. The writer accounts for 10 more in storing up possessions and another 10 in gaining wisdom. He thus concludes that two-thirds of one's years are lost to him (suggesting a normal life expectancy of 60) yet contends that the godly man will still have 60 years remaining of the days assigned by Thoth, making a round one hundred. See comments on Deuteronomy 31:2 and Isaiah 40:6–7."[2]

Moses steps into chapter 5 of Exodus, 80 years old, beyond what he believes is normal life expectancy. Yet he finally believes that God is for him and through the actions of himself and Aaron, God will to make some radical changes for the people of Israel. Moses and Aaron were hyped up on the recent call, the burning bush, and the miracles they had witnessed. They were jumping right in!

Considering the Risks

For Moses, counting the cost meant he needed to recognize what was at stake. In Egypt, he was in a position of authority, security, safety, and relative certainty. By pursuing the call of God in his life despite not really understanding the character of the God of his ancestors, he would be placing all those positions at risk. Because of this, Moses decided to execute God's call in his own strength but failed to count the cost. Without guidance or clarity from God (because he really didn't know Him yet), Moses took risks without realizing there was a greater authority available to him—he just needed to ask.

When we are in pursuit of our promises, we must count the cost. Any action taken will result in fallout—positive or negative. The wisdom of considering the risk before acting means leaning into the Lord for His guidance along the way and seeking wise counsel. In Exodus 4:18–31, we learn about the steps Moses took to begin his journey, but the context is how we can understand just how unstable his position was with the Egyptians and the Israelites. The pursuit of his life's call was a much bigger risk than we realize.

Everything Has Changed

Remember, when Moses left Egypt to serve in Jethro's household, it is because the Pharaoh was trying to have him killed. Moses had murdered an Egyptian in defense of an abused Hebrew man and fled for his own life afterward. But in Exodus 4:19, the Lord said, "Go back to Egypt, for all those who wanted to kill you are dead."

Moses packs up his family and, with the blessing from Jethro, begins the return to Egypt. But there's a common saying from author Thomas Wolfe: "You can't go home again." The Egyptian people have forgotten about Moses. Even Moses knows this Pharaoh has no idea who he is. This is not the same Egypt Moses fled from 40 years ago, and he puts a lot of energy into trying to remind God that he will not be welcome where he was raised.

Not only is Moses hesitant about returning, but he has no idea what to say when he arrives. He has lost sight of himself through 40 years of work and wonders: *What have I become?* While he used to carry favor in Egypt, that king is dead. The people from his childhood are all but gone, and he is a foreigner again returning to declare the name of a God he barely knows.

In Exodus 3:11–13, we read the conversation between God and Moses. Moses knows the Israelites will resist him. He knows the Egyptians will want him dead. God does not waver; while everything else may have changed, God's promise to the children of Israel is constant. No matter how long (or how much convincing) it takes, God is going to remain true to His word. The promises and promised land of God's people will be manifested. His people will remember who He is.

The One Who Is Always on Time

And yet, even with the direct call of God on his life, Moses was not guaranteed immediate results or an easy, safe, stable path to the promised land.

There is a gospel song I used to sing repeatedly when I first found Jesus. "He may not come when you call Him, but He'll be there right on time. He's on time God, oh yes, He is." And we see how true this is by learning about the children of Israel. Even when we look at other stories about the Hebrews in Scripture, we see the consistency of a God who shows up right on time. He makes "Plan B" better than "Plan A", and *that* we can trust.

- Abraham was promised more children than sand on the seashore (Gen. 15–17). It took approximately ten years before Sarah and Abraham had a child (Gen. 21:2–3).
- Joseph was the favorite and believed that God would make him the ruler of much (Gen. 37–40). But he was sold by his brothers, accused of rape, and put in prison before those dreams came to pass.
- Jesus Christ was sent for a special mission of deliverance, and not only did He have to grow into a man, but things had to get worse before they got better (Matt. 21).
- The disciples were commanded to preach yet were met with resistance. Jesus had to continually remind them of the gravity of which they had been chosen to participate (Matt. 10:1–22).
- Paul was led out into the wilderness after his conversion (Gal. 1:17–18).

Do not be discouraged if your promise is not immediately evident. I wonder if Moses felt discouraged watching God hardening the heart of Pharaoh time and again. Even with the foreknowledge that God would harden Pharaoh's heart, it had to be confusing to witness plague after plague and wonder when it would be enough to set God's chosen people free. But if God declares the thing, he will do the thing! God does not change His mind and He cannot lie, so if He said He would do it, you can trust Him.

Our world today is no more receptive to God's will than Pharaoh of Egypt. Our reaction to those who oppose us, or our reaction to our promise taking longer than we expect cannot be rage, offense, or surprise.

We need to cultivate a response of patience and deepening faith. This is the time to exercise your faith muscle! When doubt or frustration creeps in, change the channel of your mind. It takes effort, but it is possible. You hold the remote and you alone can choose to change your focus. It can be so discouraging but take heart! Consider Philippians 4:6–8. What true, right, and noble thing can you think of as you lean into patience in your process?

Facing the Resistance

Lastly, consider Moses's opposition. Often when we receive a word from the Lord, we can go boldly forward, excited to grow into our calling and destiny. But opposition from the outside (or even internal resistance) can quickly tire us.

READ EXODUS 5:1-9

> [1] "Afterward Moses and Aaron went to Pharaoh and said, 'This is what the Lord, the God of Israel, says: "Let my people go, so that they may hold a festival to me in the wilderness."'"
>
> [2] "Pharaoh said, 'Who is the Lord, that I should obey him and let Israel go? I do not know the Lord and I will not let Israel go.'"
>
> [3] "Then they said, 'The God of the Hebrews has met with us. Now let us take a three-day journey into the wilderness to offer sacrifices to the Lord our God, or he may strike us with plagues or with the sword.'"
>
> [4] "But the king of Egypt said, 'Moses and Aaron, why are you taking the people away from their labor? Get back to your work!' [5] Then Pharaoh said, 'Look, the people of the land are now numerous, and you are stopping them from working.'"
>
> [6] "That same day Pharaoh gave this order to the slave drivers and overseers in charge of the people: [7] 'You are no longer to supply the people with straw for making bricks; let them go and gather their own straw. [8] But require

> them to make the same number of bricks as before; don't reduce the quota. They are lazy; that is why they are crying out, "Let us go and sacrifice to our God." ⁹ Make the work harder for the people so that they keep working and pay no attention to lies.'"

Enduring the Suddenlies

Have you ever thought of pursuing your dreams and then suddenly things became much harder? Perhaps you committed to a monthly savings plan for a cash cushion during a career change, but suddenly the car needs repairs or an unexpected bill arrives. It can be disheartening to sense God calling you into an area, only to feel the door slamming in your face. But when we first entertain the idea of our God-given destiny, forces of evil will try to bring discouragement, much like they did with the children of Israel when Pharaoh removed their access to straw. Even when the enemy is prowling, take courage. God is an unchanging God. If the same resistance shows up in your story the way it did for Moses, then you are right in the pocket of where you want to be!

READ EXODUS 5:9 AGAIN:

> "Make the work harder for the people so that they keep working and pay no attention to lies."

The enemy would love to distract us from the truth of our promises. When you think about your promise, make a note of your thoughts. Is there an immediate resistance that comes to mind? Be honest with your reaction: Is the thought a lie about your promise and your future?

What would be possible in your story if the lie you are believing about your promise and the resistance between you and fulfillment of your call is not true? Today is a good day to write out the words of God, both about your calling and the truth of His character to fulfill the promise He has made over your life. Take some time to journal about a time when God has put a dream on your heart to accomplish. Maybe you're like me and have more than one. List all the dreams God has accomplished in your life and list the ones you are waiting to see become a reality.

At the end of chapters 1–5 of Exodus, Moses had received a confirmation of his calling. He had heard direction from God and was partnered with Aaron. Together they had been given authority to move into their mission of freeing the children of Israel from oppression under Pharaoh's rule.

When you find your thoughts circling back to the lie you remembered above—sowing doubt in your promise and your belief that God has a plan and a purpose for your life—think again to the promises over Abraham, Sarah, and Joseph. Remember the trials of Jesus, and the ups and downs of the disciples. Let the remembrance of their stories remind you of God's character and consistency. His timing for your life is perfect. He is a faithful God using all the chaos of the world to bring intention and direction to your life.

A Prayer

God, it is entirely possible that I have spent far too long believing lies about Your provision and the promises in my life. I am here to reject the lies that say I am too late, too old, too tired, too busy, or not enough. You are faithful and intentional to call Your children into alignment with Your heart, and You do not send them into the field without the tools they require. You equip those You call. Thank You for calling me higher, and for placing dreams in my heart that You are eager to fulfill. Amen.

Questions for Reflection

» What does God have to say about the resistance you are experiencing in your life?

» Remind yourself today of the affirmations of the call on your life. What confirmations do you have that you are in pursuit of the call of God in your life?

» If you're not sure about the call of God in your life, what does God say about the promise of who He is to you, regardless of the outcome of your story?

REMEMBER WHO HE IS

SOMETIMES, when God wants to do a new thing in our lives, we can sense a rumbling in the distance. Things begin to shift. They become uncomfortable. Things we used to be able to count on are not secure any longer. It moves us to take a step.

When we partner with the Holy Spirit and ask God to help us move forward, we can trust him to start rumbling and to provide the perfect setup for whatever is coming next.

Things were beginning to rumble for the nation of Israel. What was coming next was a shift in their lives that was so great, it would turn their world completely upside down.

MONDAY

From Bad to Worse

For the Hebrews, one day of toil blended into the next. Over the course of four centuries, the Hebrew nation had drifted and settled into a life of slavery. Even though they started out as favored family members of the second-in-command of Egypt, 400 years later their descendants were mixing bricks to build a formidable empire for the very slave masters who brutalized them. The Hebrews were living in a land they did not own, working for the benefit of a government that viewed them primarily as a labor resource.

The word *labor* in Hebrew is *abodah*—meaning "bondage" or "serve or act, labor as a slave"—and appears 20 times in the book of Exodus. When I think of laboring, I am reminded of childbirth. It may seem like the most mundane way to describe such an intense period of Israel's history, but there is nothing more poignant. Anyone connected to a pregnancy can tell you there is constant labor involved. It goes beyond the period of "active labor" when the baby is coming. As parents, as supporters, and as family members, we are always actively in the process of trying to eat correctly, prepare the home, and prepare our minds for welcoming a new family member. Labor can be beautiful, but it is often brutal: ongoing, disruptive, and tiring.

We can draw similarities to the labor of the Hebrew nation, except their outcome was nothing so miraculous as a new life. Pure survival motivated them to continue on a daily basis. But God was ready to lead them into freedom. He wasn't going to do it in a flash or with the wave of a magic wand; he was going to begin to shift the status quo and disrupt the flow that had been in place for 400 years. Change was rumbling in the distance, and it all started with Moses approaching Pharoah with a directive from the Most High God.

Pharaoh had little interest in granting any request regarding the Hebrews. He certainly did not recognize their God. After all, they were slaves. How strong could their God actually be? Pharaoh not only declined Moses's request for the Hebrews to leave, he also made the people pay for even asking.

READ EXODUS 5:10-23

[10] *"Then the slave drivers and the overseers went out and said to the people, 'This is what Pharaoh says: "I will not give you any more straw. [11] Go and get your*

own straw wherever you can find it, but your work will not be reduced at all."'
[12] *So the people scattered all over Egypt to gather stubble to use for straw.* [13] *The slave drivers kept pressing them, saying, 'Complete the work required of you for each day, just as when you had straw.'* [14] *And Pharaoh's slave drivers beat the Israelite overseers they had appointed, demanding, 'Why haven't you met your quota of bricks yesterday or today, as before?'"*

[15] *"Then the Israelite overseers went and appealed to Pharaoh: 'Why have you treated your servants this way?* [16] *Your servants are given no straw, yet we are told, "Make bricks!" Your servants are being beaten, but the fault is with your own people.'*

[17] *"Pharaoh said, 'Lazy, that's what you are—lazy! That is why you keep saying, "Let us go and sacrifice to the Lord."* [18] *Now get to work. You will not be given any straw, yet you must produce your full quota of bricks.'*

[19] *"The Israelite overseers realized they were in trouble when they were told, 'You are not to reduce the number of bricks required of you for each day.'* [20] *When they left Pharaoh, they found Moses and Aaron waiting to meet them,* [21] *and they said, 'May the Lord look on you and judge you! You have made us obnoxious to Pharaoh and his officials and have put a sword in their hand to kill us.'*

[22] *"Moses returned to the Lord and said, 'Why, Lord, why have you brought trouble on this people? Is this why you sent me?* [23] *Ever since I went to Pharaoh to speak in your name, he has brought trouble on this people, and you have not rescued your people at all.'"*

Can you feel the rumbling? Now, not only did they have to maintain their quotas, but they also had to desperately seek straw to create the bricks. The situation instantly went from bad to worse, and the Hebrews blamed Moses for their suffering.

I can imagine how Moses must have felt. He did what God told him to do, so why were things falling apart? Not only did it look like God was not rescuing His people, but now they had even more trouble to deal with. In fact, look at their response when Moses tried to encourage them with a word he received from the Lord.

READ EXODUS 6:1-9

> [1] "Then the LORD said to Moses, 'Now you will see what I will do to Pharaoh: Because of my mighty hand he will let them go; because of my mighty hand he will drive them out of his country.'
>
> [2] "God also said to Moses, 'I am the LORD. [3] I appeared to Abraham, to Isaac and to Jacob as God Almighty, but by my name the LORD I did not make myself fully known to them. [4] I also established my covenant with them to give them the land of Canaan, where they resided as foreigners. [5] Moreover, I have heard the groaning of the Israelites, whom the Egyptians are enslaving, and I have remembered my covenant.
>
> [6] "'Therefore, say to the Israelites: "I am the LORD, and I will bring you out from under the yoke of the Egyptians. I will free you from being slaves to them, and I will redeem you with an outstretched arm and with mighty acts of judgment. [7] I will take you as my own people, and I will be your God. Then you will know that I am the LORD your God, who brought you out from under the yoke of the Egyptians. [8] And I will bring you to the land I swore with uplifted hand to give to Abraham, to Isaac and to Jacob. I will give it to you as a possession. I am the LORD."'
>
> [9] "Moses reported this to the Israelites, but they did not listen to him because of their discouragement and harsh labor."

The Israelites were so overwhelmed with their own suffering and discouragement, they couldn't even trust that God had heard their groaning or remembered the promises He had made to them! And in turn, this discouraged Moses.

NOW READ VERSES 10-12

> [10] *"Then the LORD said to Moses,* [11] *'Go, tell Pharaoh king of Egypt to let the Israelites go out of his country.'*
>
> [12] *"But Moses said to the LORD, 'If the Israelites will not listen to me, why would Pharaoh listen to me, since I speak with faltering lips?'"*

Despite his hesitation, Moses would go on to obey God and start a chain of events that would lead to the freedom of the Israelites. But at the moment, I'm sure it felt impossible.

Seeing the Big Picture

Listen, friend, God's ways are not a straight path to Easy Street. We often cannot see the big picture. We often only see our own desires and our own pain. His ways are right, and true, and just, but they can be difficult. In fact, every time I have stepped out to follow a strong call from the Lord, things got harder. How's that for encouragement?!

But take courage. We serve a God who has our best interests at heart. He knows what's best for us and He has the power to make it happen. We are part of the greatest story ever told, and we can be encouraged by the struggles of the chosen people of God. We know God will fight for us in His time. The time was coming for the Lord to fight for His children, and it was going to be beyond anything they could imagine.

A Prayer

God, You have my attention. When I am allowing my heart and allegiances to wander, You have permission to regain my thoughts. You are teaching me how to realign my mind to Your Word. Help me to internalize the lessons of the Hebrews and build my own spiritual muscles to flex in the process of pursuing the promise in my life. Thank You for Your kindness in Your pursuit of me. Amen.

Questions for Reflection

» Where in your life could you use a few "training sessions" for muscle building from God?

» How can remembering who God says He is strengthen your identity?

» Has God ever used the trials of another to get your attention? How did that build your spiritual muscles?

TUESDAY

As the Veggie Tales sang, "There was a mess down in Egypt!" And what a mess it was.

But before we recount the story of the plagues and the mess each left behind, let's get real for a minute. This was much more than a mess: This was desecration. By the end, the Egyptians lived among piles of stinking, rotten corpses of frogs and lost all their crops (and ability to participate in commerce). Many more did not escape alive. God was completely ready to remove the barriers between His children and their oppressors. He had no respect for these demigods of Egypt, including the Pharaoh himself.

"Unprecedented series of disasters striking Egypt, probably culminating in the spring or early summer (*c.* 1400 BC). They struck particularly the Nile delta, although apparently not affecting the area called Goshen. These disasters were of such magnitude that the Egyptians from their earliest history could recall nothing like them (Ex. 9:24)."[1]

Why Plagues?

Throughout a few chapters of Exodus, we learn why the plagues were God's chosen method to liberate the Hebrews from captivity. With the gift of hindsight, it is easy for us to think about other ways God could have rescued the Hebrews and set them in the land promised to their ancestors. But doing so would have been like a parent intervening when their child is about ready to fall on their bike: The fall teaches them how to find their balance. The Hebrews (and the Egyptians and their Pharaoh) had much to learn about the God of creation; every person needed to know the ultimate authority of God. As each plague came upon the land and people of Egypt, it became increasingly clear that the plagues weren't random acts of nature. Moses brought the request and the warning, and there was always a powerful force behind his words that would eventually haunt and break the spirit of the leader of the Egyptians. Let's overview the plagues.

The Ten Plagues of Egypt

It should be noted that the plagues did not happen over a ten-day period. Plagues often lasted months and some historians suggest that each covered a ten-month period (say, June through the following April).

- 1st Plague, Water Turned to Blood (7:14–24)
- 2nd Plague, Frogs (7:25–8:15)
- 3rd Plague, Gnats (8:16–19)
- 4th Plague, Flies (8:20–32)

- 5th Plague, Livestock Pestilence (9:1–7)
- 6th Plague, Boils (9:8–12)
- 7th Plague, Hail and Fire (9:13–35)
- 8th Plague, Locusts (10:1–20)
- 9th Plague, Darkness (10:21–29)
- 10th Plague, Death of the Firstborn (11:1–12:30)

You may have heard about the ten plagues, but did you know that each increased in severity, targeting a specific God of the Egyptian pantheon? We will take a closer look at that soon, but in the meantime it's important to understand the impact of the plagues.

The Plagues Served Three Purposes

So the children of Israel would know who God is. *From Exodus 10:2:* "... that you may tell your children and grandchildren." The Hebrews had spent multiple generations living in Egypt, enslaved yet set apart. Still, the traditions and history of their ancestors was lost to them. The generational practice of worshiping the God of Abraham, Isaac, and Jacob was dismissed as they focused on everyday life and survival. The plagues were going to serve as a manifest reminder of their history and life as chosen children of God.

So the Egyptians would know who God is. *From Exodus 7:3–5:* "I will harden Pharaoh's heart ... Then I will lay my hand on Egypt and ... will bring out ... my people ... And the Egyptians will know that I am the Lord." The Egyptians had a laundry list of gods to appease. Imagine trying to keep each one straight in your mind, covering your bases so as not to accidentally upset the god of your flock, crops, family, or health. The first purpose of the plagues was to reveal the one true face of God to the Egyptians.

To bring God's judgment upon Egypt's gods. *From Exodus 12:12:* "On that same night I will pass through Egypt and strike down every firstborn of both people and animals, and I will bring judgment on all the gods of Egypt. I am the Lord." God was done being subtle.

The Egyptians experienced life through a maze of rituals and responses to keeping their gods appeased. The God of the Hebrews was ready to teach the Egyptians what it truly means to wield the ultimate authority of heaven and earth.

The True Safety of Goshen

The mess in Egypt, however, would completely miss the lives of the Hebrews. God's favor was upon them, even amid their oppression. How is it possible that the Israelites would experience no fallout?

The Israelites and Egyptians lived in different areas in Egypt. I imagine the area was split, with a safer part of town and a less desirable part of town (to oversimplify). Even though they were enslaved and oppressed, the Israelites specifically lived in Goshen. When Moses received direction from the Lord to go to Pharaoh after each plague, the evidence of God's favor on the Israelites was that Goshen was unaffected by the plagues. No gnats, no frogs, no lice . . . no evidence of plague or destruction in Goshen. God spared His people the suffering and loss to make it obvious to Pharaoh that His people were set apart.[2]

Goshen was close enough to Ramses for God to continually refer to the Egyptians as "your neighbors" but separated distinctly enough to leave them unaffected, proving His point that these were the children of God. Goshen was known for grazing flocks, as its western district was an irrigated plain and its eastern section was along the Mediterranean Sea. In total, it was only around 900 square miles. The location of Goshen is important to remember for when we dive into their route of the exodus later on. Take a moment to reference the location on the map in the front of this book.[3]

Offending the "Gods"

Now let's look more closely at a few of the plagues and why they were such direct assaults against the individual ruling gods of Egypt.

Water Turns to Blood: Each year, rain and melted snow dumped huge amounts of water and fine silt into the Nile. Egyptians believed that was due to Osiris, the god of the afterlife who granted life to all humans, animals, and vegetation. Osiris used the Nile to keep the land fertile. The first plague struck at the heart of the Egyptians (although some scholars also suggest that this could have been an attack on Hapi, the god of water bearing). When the water turned to blood, the Nile became useless. Between the decaying fish and the terrible stench, their source of water and bathing was destroyed.

Frogs: After the Nile was turned to blood, frogs overtook the land. The goddess Heqet (guardian of the source of the Nile River, fertility, and birth) was represented by a frog face in hieroglyphics. Geb and Nut represented the earth and the sky. They were considered the parents of Osiris, and while they were often portrayed together, Geb specifically was credited with the health and fruit of Egypt's crops. Geb oversaw the land specifically as it pertained to planting and agriculture.

Gnats: It is well known that during the months of March and April Egypt experienced massive dust storms. In Exodus 8:17, we read that God turned the dust into gnats (the translation is a little unclear and could mean lice or mosquitos, but most scholars believe gnats to be most accurate/likely). In this plague, God proved He was stronger than Geb by showing that instead of crops coming from the earth that insects would take over!

Flies: The fourth plague is interesting and we're really diving into this one. In Exodus 8:24, we read that the land was filled with flies. But in Hebrew the word is loosely translated as a small flying insect.

"The Hebrew *'arov* is literally 'swarms,' without reference to what is swarming. Most translations add a preposition and the object of the preposition, such as 'swarms of flies' or 'swarms of beetles.' In Egypt, the beetle *blatta orientalis*, arrives in late November—the approximate time of this plague—and the Egyptian word bears a close resemblance to the Hebrew. Since each plague becomes more severe and each targets an Egyptian god, one can make a strong argument for 'swarm of beetles,' or, more specifically, scarabs."[4]

Here, we recognize Khepri, a lesser solar god to Ra, who is represented by the scarab beetle in carvings, art, statues, and more. They used this specific insect due to how it rolls dung into a ball for food, much like the sun rolls daily across the sky (hence the visual metaphor). Because of this, Khepri is represented with a man's face and a scarab head.

Scarabs meant much to the Egyptians—life, protection, good health, and longevity. They were placed on amulets as jewelry, carrying a belief of Khepri's strong covering through the bearing of the objects. These amulets are frequently unearthed in ancient Egyptian temples and houses of the living. If scarabs were placed under the coffin, it was believed that no magical or spiritual force could harm the deceased.

God was challenging the very core of Egyptian belief for safety. Flies (or swarms of flying insects) were destroying the land and health of the people—the complete opposite of their purpose for worship. The scarab beetle had itself become an idol. God would have none of this.

God destroyed the livestock of the Egyptians, laughing at Apis/Hathor, the bull deity worshiped as crucial to the strength of Egypt. When God sent the plague to destroy the Egyptian's livestock, he wasn't trying to destroy their agricultural strength. The Apis/Hathor bull head in hieroglyphics represented the God Hathor. God was showing He was stronger than this god that represented strength for the Egyptians. God covered the Egyptians in boils, mocking Sekhmet, daughter of Ra, and her inability to truly create or end epidemics. Some scholars also suggest this was an attack against Isis, the goddess of medicine and peace. Either way, the plague pronounced the Egyptians as unclean, a complete affront to a society obsessed with beauty and cleanliness.

Unrelenting Devastation
READ EXODUS 9:13-24

With each plague, the devastation grew. When hail destroyed the crops, remaining livestock, and even the workers in the fields, the Egyptians cried out to their goddess Nut. But she was powerless to influence the sky. It seems that all that remained of this great empire was waste. And then, the locusts descended (Ex. 10:1–20).

"The devastation brought by locusts is hard to imagine. One square mile of a swarm contains from 100,000,000 to 200,000,000 locusts, and swarms typically cover as much as 400 square miles. Each locust eats its own body weight daily, and they strip a country bare, leaving millions of people in famine for years.

"The cumulative force of the plagues has had a devastating effect on Egypt, its people and its economy: the land lies buried beneath a putrid mass of decaying fish and frogs; the livestock have been felled by anthrax; the crops have been destroyed by hail and fire; disease and infections have ravaged the people—and now Egypt faces an onslaught of locusts."[5]

Seth was the god of storms and disorder. The plague of locusts felt like a one-up: an affront to Seth as if to say, "You think you can bring disorder to the land? Watch me." And even as the locusts ravaged what little remained in the land, Ra was brought to task through the plague of darkness (Ex. 10:21–29).

Removing What Alienates You

God methodically and ruthlessly undermined the authority and respect for every single god worshiped in Egypt. Each plague is a demonstration of God's ultimate strength and a desecration of the religious structure of Egypt. And they provide clarity to all who witness the aftermath: the Israelites, the Egyptians, and Pharaoh himself.

But let's stop for a moment and consider how this scene is impacting the Hebrews. The religious system of the Egyptians has become the underlying culture of the day for them. Over the generations, they have adopted customs outside of their lineage. They have lost sight of their ancestral promises and in turn become alienated from their God. But He has a plan to bring them back to Himself.

Pharaoh's stubborn resistance remains, as he thinks that surely the worst is over. But nothing could be further from the truth. What comes next will destroy his confidence and rock his identity to the core.

A Prayer

God, I give You permission to alienate anything that takes the place of You in my life. Show me when I resist, and why. Give me strength to follow Your lead and leave behind the idols that have provided me with a false sense of security. May I find refuge beneath the shadow of Your wings, and may my obedience bring You joy as I follow You today.

Questions for Reflection

» Where do you see demigods and idols getting involved in your beliefs about God?

» Is there a roadblock alienating you from your ability to grow in your trust of God?

» Does your promise require you to increase in your faith?

» Remind yourself of a time when God revealed an idol to you; then thank Him for teaching you how to remove it.

WEDNESDAY

The Last God Standing

Egypt looked like a wasteland. The rot and filth that were left after the first six plagues had been further ravaged by the locusts. The mighty Nile, the symbol of the favor of the gods, now flowed with sickness and despair. Methodically, one by one, the God of the Hebrews had brought judgment aimed at the gods of the Egyptians. Besides Pharaoh himself, who was considered a god, there was one major deity left. Ra. The god of the sun. To the Egyptians, as long as the sun was still shining, their god Ra still sat on his throne.

And then, the unthinkable happened. The sky went dark. Fear and dread filled every corner of Egypt, hope left the land, and still Pharaoh stood firm. Each Pharaoh believed that he was a god, appointed to rule over the people. By that logic, the firstborn son was also considered to be a god. Pharaoh was not just another name for "king"—it was another name for God.

He, a god in a long line of ruling gods, stood alone in the dark and would not bow to the Lord of the Hebrews.

"The sun, the most worshipped God in Egypt other than Pharaoh himself, gave no light. The Lord showed that he had control over the sun as a witness that the God of Israel had ultimate power over life and death. The psychological and religious impact would have had a profound influence on the Egyptians at this point. Darkness was a representation of death, judgment and hopelessness. Darkness was a complete absence of light."[6]

The Final Plague

According to Egyptian beliefs, to be a Pharaoh was to be a god. This title was passed down from father to son, from generation to generation. The final plague was sent to destroy the Pharaoh's firstborn son.

I don't want to take too much liberty with Scripture, but I can picture Pharaoh in all his splendor waking up the morning of the tenth plague, lamenting the loss in his land, but determined to stay the course. And then, the news reached his ears. His son, his heir, had died. He rushed to his child's lifeless body, horrified at the sudden loss. The wailing of Egyptian mothers must have shaken the palace walls with torment. Can you imagine the sound? The volume? In their hearts, as Egyptians throughout the land held the bodies of their dead children, they were all wondering the same question. *Who was this God to Moses, this God of Israel who continued to harass them?*

This scene sent Pharaoh from utter sadness as a father into rage over the loss of Egypt's next king. However, it also exposed his humanity. Clearly, he was not invincible as he may have previously believed. Indeed, the God of the children of Israel showed him exactly how human he truly was, and how powerless his efforts were against the God of heaven.

A Prayer

God, You are the sovereign Lord over all. In Your wisdom, You allow and invite my thoughts to wander over what You are doing without always giving me clarity at the forefront. Thank You for giving me an opportunity to trust what You are doing without seeing the full picture. I confess that sometimes, I have questioned Your judgment in allowing those positioned against me to remain unscathed. Thank You for releasing me from carrying and executing judgment. May my heart continue to remain soft and tender toward Your ways and Your wisdom. Amen.

Questions for Reflection

>> In what way has your promise been clouded by your own expectations of what it should look like?

» How can you pursue a greater intimacy with God and knowledge of your own identity even while waiting for the promise to arise?

» Are there any areas where you've been leaning on your own understanding of truth instead of the wisdom of the Lord?

THURSDAY

READ EXODUS 12:1-26

Celebration: First Steps

When I was younger, I dated a man who lived in London, England. He invited me to move in with him. I was still so young in my faith, and I knew my convictions to avoid cohabitation before marriage would not stand up against the chance to live in another country. It was not long after that the Lord started dealing with me. After months of turmoil, I heard the Lord tell me it was time to go home. But rather than obeying and making arrangements, I wanted confirmation (in case I wasn't hearing God correctly).

Part of my hesitation came from my lifestyle; I was a young, single mother living the high life in London. The recession in the USA hit my parents hard, with both losing their employment. Surely, I must be hearing God wrong—did He really want me to leave London behind and return to a small lumber town, couch surfing? With the economy at a low, I figured I would quickly be on state financial support and unable to find a job. I decided to dig in and argue with God.

The Lord told me to read Psalm 34. As I read, verse 10 stood out to me: "The lions may grow weak and hungry, but those who seek the Lord lack no good thing." Well, if that wasn't specific! Still, I sought more confirmation. I prayed fervently that I would hear a word from God at the next Sunday morning service.

When I arrived at church, I was floored. The pastor of seventeen years announced to his congregation that he was returning to America in pursuit of God's call upon his life. Actually, his entire sermon was about the call of God in our lives and occupying the land you've been called into.

You might think, after all this, that returning to my hometown would be an easy decision. I could clearly hear God's heart, and knew I wanted to honor Him. However, the idea of choosing homelessness after living with such physical provision was one of the hardest decisions I've ever made. Yet even in my early stages of faith, I found strength to believe that a chance on God is a chance on a sure thing—even when I am unsure. My role was simply to take the first steps and prepare for the journey. He would handle the rest.

God Calls the Hebrews to Prepare

Let's backtrack just a little. We already visited the scene in Pharaoh's room when he learned of his son's death. We already pictured the wave of sorrow that spread throughout Egypt as families were waking to the loss of their firstborn children.

But how God was preparing and protecting His people before the final plague swept through the land? He directed them exactly how and when to slaughter a goat or a sheep. And then He explained what to do next.

READ EXODUS 12:7-13

> [7] *"Then they are to take some of the blood and put it on the sides and tops of the doorframes of the houses where they eat the lambs. [8] That same night they are to eat the meat roasted over the fire, along with bitter herbs, and bread made without yeast. [9] Do not eat the meat raw or boiled in water, but roast it over a fire—with the head, legs and internal organs. [10] Do not leave any of it till morning; if some is left till morning, you must burn it. [11] This is how you are to eat it: with your cloak tucked into your belt, your sandals on your feet and your staff in your hand. Eat it in haste; it is the Lord's Passover.*
>
> [12] *"On that same night I will pass through Egypt and strike down every firstborn of both people and animals, and I will bring judgment on all the gods of Egypt. I am the Lord. [13] The blood will be a sign for you on the houses where you are, and when I see the blood, I will pass over you. No destructive plague will touch you when I strike Egypt."*

The Lord spoke to the Israelites and told them to prepare before they started the celebration. Part of this preparation became an important event that would live on through Hebrew generations: the Passover. The blood on the doorposts was a sign to the angel of death that this was a chosen home of God's children. They could not touch it. The role of the Israelites during this time was simply to take the first steps in preparation for their journey—and God would handle the rest.

➤ What type of food did the Lord have the children of Israel prepare?

» Why do you think the Lord wanted them to prepare this specific type of food?

» How often were the children supposed to eat this food and remember this day? (hint Exodus: 12:24)

Peace in the Waiting

Can you imagine waiting all night while the people around you were dying? Exodus 11:6 and 12:30 tells us that they could hear the wailing throughout the land. Imagine sitting in their homes, listening to the heart cries of their families and neighbors, as the midnight hour approached. What anxieties were they experiencing? *Did I put enough blood on the doorposts? Could the Angel of Death see it well enough? What if Moses was wrong?*

Here they were, oppressed and enslaved, living in harsh conditions for hundreds of years. Suddenly, a glimmer of hope to enter the land promised to their ancestors finally arrives. Could it be real? They witnessed the plagues and miracles wreak havoc on their neighbors, while leaving themselves unscathed. Could it finally be their time to reach Canaan?

LET'S REVISIT EXODUS 6:4-5 (AMP)

> [4] *I also established My covenant with them, to give them the land of Canaan, the land in which they lived as strangers (temporary residents, foreigners). [5] And I have also heard the groaning of the sons of Israel, whom the Egyptians have*

> *enslaved, and I have faithfully remembered My covenant (with Abraham, Isaac, and Jacob).*

Consider the uncertainties from your own life. The first time you committed your life to the Lord or took the first step toward a long-awaited dream. Maybe worry and anxiety were high, keeping you awake at night. Will you be able to pay the bills and provide for your children if you quit your job? It's not where you are meant to be, but technically, it's provision. Will your abusive husband find you if you dare to try and run in the night? Did you hear God correctly when you made that life-changing decision? Will financial aid cover the classes you just signed up to take? Would going into rehab affect your children for that year or would it solidify a longer promise of a happy sober life for years to come?

You've come so far stepping out in faith. Don't stop now.

Let's cultivate some peace in our spirits for the waiting. Like the Israelites, we may hear things that make us afraid or uncertain before our promise arrives and celebration takes place. Take some time to talk to God about those nerve-racking, life-changing decisions you may have made in your past. Journal what God is saying to you at this moment. Is He reminding you of His plans and promises for you? Is He reminding you how He came through every single time? Maybe this obstacle that sits in front of you today should stand as a reminder of ALL that He can do, has done, and will do in your life. Let these scriptural promises be a reminder of the confidence you can carry.

- No weapon formed against you shall prosper.
- You can do all things through Christ who gives you strength.
- Lean not on your own understanding but in all your ways acknowledge him and He'll make your path straight.
- You are a new creation in Christ, old things have passed away.

- And let us be transformed by the renewing of our minds.
- If He took care of you while you still were in sin, how much more now? Does a robin not worry about what it will eat? So, you do not need to worry about a thing.
- Be anxious for nothing, but in all things with prayer and supplication, let your requests be known and the peace that surpasses all understanding will guard your heart and mind.

Research professor and Bible commentator John Oswalt says, "God allowed his people to be maneuvered into a situation from which there was no possible human escape. But in that hour, God delivered them in a way that would not only shape Israelite faith but also Christian faith as well throughout all the centuries to come."[7]

READ EXODUS 12:23-27 (AMP)

> [23] "For the LORD will pass through to strike the Egyptians; and when He sees the blood on the lintel [above the entryway] and on the two doorposts, the LORD will pass over the door and will not allow the destroyer to come into your houses to slay you. [24] You shall observe this event [concerning Passover] as an ordinance for you and for your children forever. [25] When you enter the land which the LORD will give you, as He has promised, you shall keep and observe this service. [26] When your children say to you, 'What does this service mean to you?' [27] you shall say, 'It is the sacrifice of the Lord's Passover, for He passed over the houses of the Israelites in Egypt when He struck the Egyptians, but spared our houses.' And the people bowed [their heads] low and worshiped [God]."

God promises us that the destroyer will not be permitted to enter our homes. He instructs us to remember the promises and what He has done. What promises do you need to remember? Are there important dates in your past you can bring to mind? Maybe you need to remember the first time you earned a one-year clean and sober chip, or the day you surrendered your life to Christ. What about the day you returned to God like the prodigal son? What reason made you march out of your Egypt to never look back? These small steps of celebration may become the victory stories you carry as testimonies for your children someday.

Remind them of the resiliency in their lineage—the struggle and the faith it took for you to find the land you occupy today (physically and in the Spirit).

Pharaoh Concedes

So we've taken a quick look back at how the Hebrews prepared and protected their households, and now we revisit Pharaoh. The death of his son, whom he had believed to be a god, had rocked him to his core. History tells us that from the time of his birth, the Egyptians were already building Pharaoh's tomb to prepare him for the afterlife.

Pharaoh was devastated, and in his grief, horror, and rage, he ordered the Hebrews to leave his realm.

READ EXODUS 12:28-33 (NLT)

> [28] "So the people of Israel did just as the Lord had commanded through Moses and Aaron. [29] And that night at midnight, the Lord struck down all the firstborn sons in the land of Egypt, from the firstborn son of Pharaoh, who sat on his throne, to the firstborn son of the prisoner in the dungeon. Even the firstborn of their livestock were killed. [30] Pharaoh and all his officials and all the people of Egypt woke up during the night, and loud wailing was heard throughout the land of Egypt. There was not a single house where someone had not died. [31] Pharaoh sent for Moses and Aaron during the night. 'Get out!' he ordered. 'Leave my people—and take the rest of the Israelites with you! Go and worship the Lord as you have requested. [32] Take your flocks and herds, as you said, and be gone. Go,

but bless me as you leave.' [33] All the Egyptians urged the people of Israel to get out of the land as quickly as possible, for they thought, 'We will all die!'"

Think about a time God pointed you in an obvious direction. Did He open or close a door? Did an opportunity end suddenly, but a new level of clarity arose? These moments in our lives should be instances when we celebrate God's faithfulness, direction, and guidance. This is one of the ways He shows us how special we are and how glorious His plans for us are. We learn that we can rely on His guidance and direction. These occasions are rarely an audible moment, with "Thus sayeth the Lord!" booming from the sky. It is the prompting of our conscience, or a question or word of encouragement from someone in our lives.

When writing about doors opening in our lives American author, educator, and activist Parker Palmer says, "But a lot of way has closed behind me, and that's had the same guiding effect."[8]

Take a moment to thank God for the way He closed a door behind you. Is there a time He removed an opportunity that led to reformation in your story? Let it become an anniversary and celebration! Write those moments down. Frame them or put them in a keepsake jar. We cannot forget all that God has done for us. In fact, in our lowest moments of confidence and clarity, it was a true gift to have these memories written out for our remembrance.

From the work I do now—assisting in the escapes of women and their children leaving their traffickers (some call this rescue)—I could share countless stories of women being forced out of their prisons by the very people who enslaved them.

Taking the first steps toward our promised land can be scary. Equally terrifying are the first steps away from a dangerous situation, even when we know we need to leave. But when we don't move swiftly enough, God will step in.

Psalm 40:1–12 (MSG) gives me so much comfort in reminding me that God has a plan and He can be trusted. Circle and then rewrite which verse stands out to you the most:

---

¹⁻³ I waited and waited and waited for GOD.
*   At last he looked; finally he listened.*
He lifted me out of the ditch,
*   pulled me from deep mud.*
He stood me up on a solid rock
*   to make sure I wouldn't slip.*
He taught me how to sing the latest God-song,
*   a praise-song to our God.*
More and more people are seeing this:
*   they enter the mystery,*
*   abandoning themselves to God.*
⁴⁻⁵ Blessed are you who give yourselves over to GOD,
*   turn your backs on the world's "sure thing,"*
*   ignore what the world worships;*
The world's a huge stockpile
*   of GOD-wonders and God-thoughts.*
Nothing and no one
*   comes close to you!*
I start talking about you, telling what I know,
*   and quickly run out of words.*
Neither numbers nor words
⁶ Doing something for you, bringing something to you—
*   that's not what you're after.*
Being religious, acting pious—
*   that's not what you're asking for.*
You've opened my ears
*   so I can listen.*
⁷⁻⁸ So I answered, "I'm coming.

I read in your letter what you wrote about me,
And I'm coming to the party
you're throwing for me."
That's when God's Word entered my life,
became part of my very being.
9-10 *I've preached you to the whole congregation,*
I've kept back nothing, GOD—you know that.
I didn't keep the news of your ways
a secret, didn't keep it to myself.
I told it all, how dependable you are, how thorough.
I didn't hold back pieces of love and truth
For myself alone. I told it all,
let the congregation know the whole story.
11-12 *Now GOD, don't hold out on me,*
don't hold back your passion.
Your love and truth
are all that keeps me together.
When troubles ganged up on me,
a mob of sins past counting,
I was so swamped by guilt
I couldn't see my way clear.
More guilt in my heart than hair on my head,
so heavy the guilt that my heart gave out.

A Prayer

God, You have been directing my steps since the beginning. In Your kindness and wisdom, You draw me closer to my promise even through my own resistance. Thank You for providing the steps, one at a time, to show me the path to my promised land. Your love and truth are all that keep me together. May my faith and growing intimacy in relationship with You continue to bolster my steps; I've come so far toward this promise. Don't let me be held back now! Amen.

Questions for Reflection

» Why do you think Pharaoh responded with a request for a blessing as he sent the Hebrews out?

» Have you ever had an emotional response to something horrific happening in your life?

» Describe a time that God made it that obvious for you to make a move.

FRIDAY

The Departure
READ ISAIAH 49:1-2

> [1] "Listen to me, you islands; hear this, you distant nations: Before I was born the Lord called me; from my mother's womb he has spoken my name. [2] He made my mouth like a sharpened sword, in the shadow of his hand, he hid me; he made me into a polished arrow and concealed me in his quiver."

Archery is an incredible skill, and a dangerous one at that. In untrained hands, the arrow can fly off-course, causing wild and irreparable harm.

In the Scripture above, the term *quiver* is significant because there are many types of quivers in existence. In some eras, arrows were bundled in a quiver that was carried on the back of the archer. Quivers can also be strapped to the body so that the arrow can easily be grabbed and held in the hand of the archer. My personal favorite, however, is the placement of a quiver during warfare when an archer has a fixed location. In this case, he keeps his quiver at his feet so he can pull an arrow from it and send it to its destination. What a beautiful picture—before we can be sent out, we must get to the feet of the one sending us.

God requires us to engage in our own acts of freedom. We're not simply inanimate arrows, waiting to be thrust through the air toward our destiny. We know some of the Hebrews continually grumbled on their way out of Egypt, leaving only because the door was shut and they were kicked out! It is hard to imagine a scenario where we might choose to remain enslaved.

But when we stay in situations that are comfortable, instead of stepping into the unknown, it can often be because of fear. Other times it is because we have developed character habits that we just can't seem to break. God desires our partnership; He is a loving Father, inviting us to participate in our own process toward freedom. To become refined, sharpened, and trained as a willing arrow in His quiver. One thing is certain: Getting yourself to the feet of Jesus, ushering the Spirit of the God of this universe into your home, and into your prayer life will radically change you. It will break off fear; it will give you strategic direction; it will alter habits and give you a heart of flesh. We are never sent flying through the air alone or without a target to hit.

God had an intended target for the Hebrew nation, and it wasn't in Egypt.

READ EXODUS 12:33-49 (AMP)

> [33] *"The Egyptians anxiously urged the people to leave, to send them out of the land quickly, for they said, 'We will all be dead.'"*

God sometimes has to force us out of situations when we would rather stay put. I love the Jars of Clay song, "I'd rather feel the pain that's all too familiar than be broken by a lover I don't understand." Even though most Israelites wanted to leave Egypt, some truly wanted to remain. This was their home, their birthplace, their ancestors' roots. They didn't know what was waiting for them in Canaan, and so some of them went solely because God shut a door and kicked them out. Yet they soon discovered God had a plan to provide them with exactly what they needed for the journey.

> 34 "So the people took their dough before it was leavened, their kneading bowls being bound up in their clothes on their shoulders. 35 Now the Israelites had acted in accordance with the word of Moses; and they had asked the Egyptians for articles of silver and articles of gold, and clothing. 36 The LORD gave the people favor in the sight of the Egyptians, so that they gave them what they asked. And so, they plundered the Egyptians [of those things]."

Even without any external setbacks, this journey would have taken months. They needed supplies to trade, to buy supplies, and how would they do that leaving as slaves with nothing? It was through the Egyptians that God once again proved faithful, showing He is the King who provides for His children.

> 37 "Now the Israelites journeyed from Rameses to Succoth, about six hundred elaphs of foot soldiers, besides [the women and] the children. 38 A mixed multitude [of non-Israelites from foreign nations] also went with them, along with both flocks and herds, a very large number of livestock. 39 And they baked unleavened cakes of the dough which they brought from Egypt; it was not leavened, since they were driven [quickly] from Egypt and could not delay, nor had they prepared any food for themselves."

The journey out of Egypt proper was just the beginning. The children of Israel were about to travel along "The King's Highway," a trade route of vital importance in the ancient Near East, connecting Africa to Mesopotamia. Imagine knowing you were on your way out the door with nothing to offer, and this to look forward to:

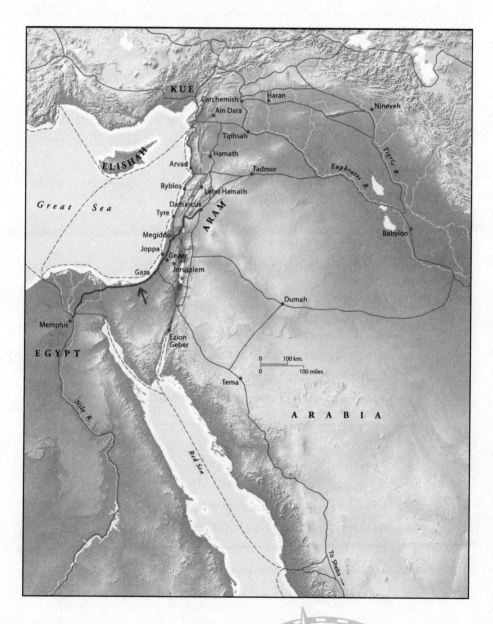

"The King's Highway (Derech HaMelech) is referred to in the Book of Numbers (Numbers 20:17, 21:22), where it is related that the Israelites, in their Exodus journey needed to use the road. They had left from Kadesh, and requested the right of way from the King of Edom but were refused passage. He vowed he would attack them if they used the road. They even offered to pay for any water their cattle drank. Still the King of Edom refused them passage and advanced against them with a large and heavily armed force. After making a detour and coming to the Transjordan area between River Arnon and River Jabbok, they made the same request to Amorite King Sihon, and for the second time on the same road they were denied passage and King Sihon engaged them in battle at Jahaz, where they won that battle 'by the edge of the sword.' As a result, they gained control in that land and to the north of it. The tribes of Manasseh (eastern half), Gad, and Reuben subsequently settled those territories."[9]

Provisions from the Enemy
NOW LET'S LOOK AGAIN AT VERSES 35-36 (AMP)

> [35] "Now the Israelites had acted in accordance with the word of Moses; and they had asked the Egyptians for articles of silver and articles of gold, and clothing. [36] The Lord gave the people favor in the sight of the Egyptians, so that they gave them what they asked. And so, they plundered the Egyptians [of those things]."

Can you imagine asking your neighbors for riches on your way out of the city after all that had happened? When all you've known of these people is that they passively (or directly) have benefitted from your enslavement, you are told by God to power up and ask them to hand over their wealth. Through this big request, God reminds us that obedience to His command leads to readiness, which leads to provision for our journeys. Whatever you are going through now or whatever you have been through, trust that not only does God have a plan for your life, but He is going to provide the way. Another interesting fact about the riches gained: Israel inherited plunder at its prime—a legacy the ancient world had yet attained anywhere else. Further proof that God was preparing His children with a foundation of provision and security.

Take a minute to meditate on the following verses. What do they reveal to you about the nature of God and the way He sets a target before you?

READ JEREMIAH 29:11-13

> [11] "For I know the plans I have for you," declares the LORD, "plans to prosper you and not to harm you, plans to give you hope and a future. [12] Then you will call on me and come and pray to me, and I will listen to you. [13] You will seek me and find me when you seek me with all your heart."

READ 1 CORINTHIANS 2:9

> "However, as it is written: 'What no eye has seen, what no ear has heard, and what no human mind has conceived—the things God has prepared for those who love him."

Delivered with a Purpose

"GOD'S GOAL IS NOT MERELY DELIVERANCE BUT RELATIONSHIP."
—John Oswalt[10]

READ EXODUS 12:42-49 (AMP)

> ^{42} *"It is a night of watching to be observed for the* Lord *for having brought them out of the land of Egypt; this same night is for the* Lord, *to be observed and celebrated by all the Israelites throughout their generations.*
>
> ^{43} *"The* Lord *said to Moses and Aaron, "This is the ordinance of the Passover: no foreigner is to eat it;* ^{44} *but every man's slave who is bought with money, after you have circumcised him, then he may eat it.* ^{45} *No stranger (temporary resident, foreigner) or hired servant shall eat it.* ^{46} *It is to be eaten inside one house; you shall not take any of the meat outside the house, nor shall you break any of its bones.* ^{47} *The entire congregation of Israel shall keep and celebrate it.* ^{48} *If a stranger living temporarily among you wishes to celebrate the Passover to the* Lord, *all his males must be circumcised, and then he may participate and celebrate it like one that is born in the land. But no uncircumcised person may eat it.* ^{49} *The same law shall apply to the native-born and to the stranger who lives temporarily among you."*

I find it interesting that the way that they knew who wanted to be in relationship with God and their newfound identity was through circumcision. I can easily identify areas in my heart that I have cried out to God to circumcise. Gossiping, anger, frustration, backbiting, lust—you name it I did it. Still do. I needed to start celebrating my freedom from these character hang ups and walk into who I truly *wanted* to become.

Are there areas in your life that are stopping you from walking into a deeper relationship with God? Don't worry. There is no judgment here. God knows you. He knows your habits from years of living within your culture. He knows about any trauma or abuses you may have suffered as a child and the effect they've had on your mind and actions. He understands the impact far beyond what even you or I can comprehend. He knows you are human and, regardless of the areas where you struggle, He still saw fit to send for your rescue, to lift you from your bondage and point you toward freedom. He didn't leave you in the middle of your sin and He surely isn't starting now.

We read these encouraging words as Exodus chapter 12 concludes:

> [50] *"Then all the Israelites did so; they did just as the Lord had commanded Moses and Aaron.* [51] *And on that very same day the Lord brought the Israelites out of the land of Egypt by their hosts (tribal armies)."*

He gave them a fresh start, and He has done the same for you. Let's trust that He is the faithful God He has always been and start walking toward our promised land!

Restoration to Right Relationship

"The Exodus is really about becoming rightly related to God. Over 50 verses are given over to discussion of worship practices . . . The author is proving his point. Even if these slaves manage to escape their oppressors, they will have missed the point of the event unless they surround their memories of it with appropriate acts of worship. The question for humans is not whether we will serve a master but only WHAT master will we serve? If we live our lives in service to our creator, we will be free to be all we were made to be. If we refuse that service, we are seeking to live in ways we were never made for, and the result will be a worse bondage than we ever dreamed, whether to own our own self will or to the will of another."[11]

Throughout every step of the way, God has instructed Moses and given the children of Israel clarity about His character and intentions for their lives. He reminds them time and again that He is willing to remove any barrier and to use any missteps to His glory. As the children start to obey, their relationship to God also changes course. They are watching miracles break forth and learning how to lean into the unknown, despite the enormity of what could happen.

But this is the God who desires our obedience over all else. We read in James 4:17 that to know what is right and choose not to do it is a sin. In our lives, we have a choice every day to pursue the call of God, no matter the cost. We also have the choice to ignore it and move in our own confidence.

A Prayer

God, show me the areas of my life where You are calling me into greater obedience. Your character is more complex than I can understand, but You are so kind in bringing me closer to Your heart through all my trials. Remind me of the roadblocks You have faithfully removed from my path. Thank You for continuing to provide for my journey and give me clarity of purpose. Your steady hand is leading me toward a target and promise where I can give You proper glory—keep my heart praising You all along the way! Amen.

Questions for Reflection

» Are you moving in an area of life that makes you want to sing/rejoice/express gratitude?

» What are you practicing that moves you closer toward that area of life or further from it?

» Can God trust you with this area of life and big requests of obedience?

» Have you become a grumbler along the way when things seem unsteady or out of control?

LESSON FOUR

REMEMBER YOUR STRENGTH

READ EXODUS 13:1-17:16

Can you trust that God is kind as He calls you into an unknown desert journey toward a new land? From one season into something new? It's a valid question. Even when God gives us the green light to move forward toward His promise, it doesn't mean that we have everything we need to settle into new territory yet. We often need to build strength and character that is needed for the next season. God always builds character in us along the way, and the lessons we learn will play a vital part in breaking the cycles that keep us moving in circles.

We see this play out as the Israelites leave Egypt for the promised land. As we studied at the end of lesson 3, God provided the Hebrews with resources for the journey, and those resources came from the very population that had enslaved them.

When we talk about strengthening ourselves, we must consider three areas of our character that hold us up: faith, agency, and resiliency. We are going to unpack these topics in the lives of the children of Israel, but as you're reading the rest of this lesson, I want you to consider how your faith, agency, and resiliency are impacting your daily life and travels into your promised land. Our agency is the actions *we* take to create a certain outcome. Like Moses, are you able to throw the staff on the ground in partnership with God when He asks you to step out and do something you've never heard or seen? In the face of great danger, can you invoke resiliency to remain steadfast and focused when the enemy of your life is chasing you toward the ocean with no boats in sight?

It's time to admit that if nothing changes, then nothing changes. But friends, we are not alone in our trials or in building our strength and character, and neither were the children of Israel. Let's move on by studying Exodus 13–17.

MONDAY

READ EXODUS 13:1-22

Knowledge of the Road Ahead

Thankfully, God knows the road ahead of us. He is the originator of the promise, the prophetic word, and the land we will occupy. He knows what lies ahead for the children of Israel, and so He tells them to remember. In Hebrew, the word *remember* is *zakar*. It means to "recall to mind." God wanted His children to recall all that He has done for them and for their ancestors.

The road that lay ahead was going to require the children of Israel to continually recount the miracles of God. It would take a lot of faith and confidence in God's call to follow a pillar of fire through the sky at night. It sounds so miraculous and mundane at the same time—yet in the moment, I imagine it was overwhelming and inspiring . . . until the Hebrews grew weary.

I have been holding on to a dream for about six years since the Lord started opening doors. It has not been an easy promise to hold on to— something that only God could do. Every time I heard a no, or a door shut, I wanted to cry. But a fire inside me wouldn't allow it. I remembered the doors that opened in previous seasons; I remembered the prophetic word from a stranger. I would close my eyes any time I got weary or doubted, lean on the fire on the inside, and recall what God had already spoken. He cannot lie. He cannot partner with sin, so if He says He will do it, He will keep His promise. Keep following the fire.

Maybe you are in a similar situation, working toward a promise that feels stale in this season. Have you been following a pillar of fire for days unending? It makes sense that you might grow weary in these seasons, but this is what it looks like to build your faith. These are the best moments to stir your memory and recall what God has done for you and your life! Something happens to our foundation when we are in the middle of a storm and God suddenly intervenes and alters our course. Think about a time when God showed up for you and you experienced an explosion of confidence in your faith. Remember: We are on a journey out of our past bondage and the excuses that have kept us from our promises. This is when *you* must recall the miracles of God in your own life as a reminder that He is faithful to His word.

Israel Has a Future

Why would God tell them to consecrate firstborn children and livestock? He wanted them to remember! It is so crucial in our walk to remember what He has done. He did not ask them to consecrate firstborns when they were still in Egypt, but He instructed them to do it once they reached the promised land (13:11–16). Why do you think that is? Have you had times when God has done something for you that makes you want to please Him? Like any relationship, it is reciprocal, and this was God's first step at the beginning to build a relationship with His people.

Think about the way God has asked you to partner with Him in shaping your future. What traditions has He given you? Do you have specific habits that are daily or weekly actions to honor God in the process of occupying your promise? What tasks or moments will you consecrate this week? Where will you invite God into the driver's seat and allow His higher agenda to dictate your story?

Shaping the Future

"Israel had a future, and God was concerned about the shape of that future."[1]

The journey to begin creating new habits and building relationships with their "new" God had just begun and it would take time to learn His ways, hear His voice, and fully trust Him. It would take time to develop new spiritual muscles.

READ EXODUS 13:17-18

> [17] "When Pharaoh let the people go, God did not lead them on the road through the Philistine country, though that was shorter. For God said, 'If they face war, they might change their minds and return to Egypt.' [18] So God led the people around by the desert road toward the Red Sea. The Israelites went up out of Egypt ready for battle."

Let's look at the map again, focusing on the Philistine country that this portion of Scripture is referring to. The route from Goshen to Canaan was literally an Egyptian fortress.

"GOD KNEW THE LIMITED PERSPECTIVES AND NAÏVE EXPECTATIONS FULL WELL AND THUS LED THE CHILDREN OF ISRAEL AWAY FROM THE PHILISTINE TERRITORY."

—Douglas Stuart[2]

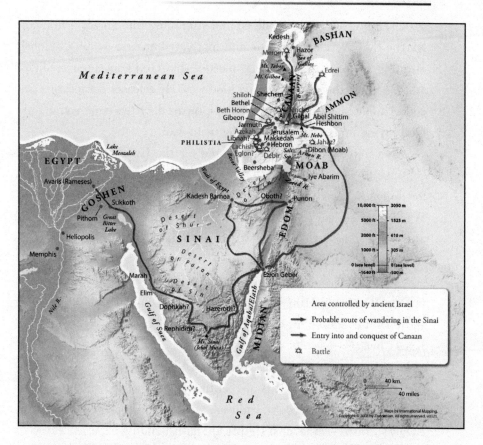

One of the first places the children of Israel would pass through is Rameses. Ramses was a "store city," a city that housed war materials to fight off invasion.[3] The Philistine territory was known as a heavily armed military road. Tents and weapon housing areas lined the pass. The Israelites, despite their newfound unity of heart and purpose, were not ready for a war with a people group of this magnitude. The Philistines were an army looking to expand their territory and the Israelites were not yet seen as a people group. They were not even regarded as a nation until 1230 BC.[4]

Trusting God for the Change

What do you think might have happened to the Israelites if they would have moved before they were ready? I imagine seeing this rag-tag

111

group fleeing Egypt, bewildered and stumbling into an accidental war. Maybe they were enthusiastic and motivated at first—even anxiously awaiting a chance to prove their mettle—but God knows our readiness and He knew theirs, too. In His kindness, He releases compassion and concern for us, even when we are unprepared. Often what sounds like God saying no is really God asking us to wait.

God's concern for our future (and for the Israelites') is that if we continue to white-knuckle the steering wheel, we will continue to fight for things we are not called to battle with our own short-lived strength. What if Israel had resisted the long way around and pushed to travel along Via Maris? I don't know if they would have had the courage to continue once their initial adrenaline rush wore off.

"God maneuvered his people into a place where they could do nothing else but trust Him. The next move of God was one of the most significant events in all of the biblical faith next to the resurrection of Jesus Christ."[5]

Maybe, like the Israelites, you're in a place where you can do nothing else but trust God. It is also entirely possible that the crossroads before you—the trial you've endured, where you slipped right from the enemy's grasp—is the most significant faith-building experience of your life so far.

So why didn't God choose to simply defeat the Philistines on behalf of the children of Israel? He released them from Pharaoh's rule, so wouldn't another victory be in line with His character? It would have been a meaningless victory. The Philistines, to this point in history, had nothing to do with the Hebrews. Starting a war or subduing them as the enemy would have become barely a footnote in history of the Israelites. Instead, we now have the story of David to remember.

Essentially, if the children of Israel had taken the short route, they would have encountered multiple high-risk situations they were unprepared to overcome. By guiding them along the longer route, God instructed the children of Israel and brought them into development.

They became prepared for their new lives and transitioned into a people who would be able to truly occupy the land after arrival.

Details Fulfilled
READ EXODUS 13:19

> *"Moses took the bones of Joseph with him because Joseph had made the Israelites swear an oath. He had said, 'God will surely come to your aid, and then you must carry my bones up with you from this place.'"*

Elaborate care was taken with Joseph's bones because of the conversation between Moses and Joseph before the latter's death. This short exchange revealed that God's plan to bring His children to the promised land was always meant to be. It was a sign that what God had promised was going to come to pass—that their exodus from Egypt was the fulfillment of a historical prophecy, not simply a plan by Aaron and Moses to escape their enslavement.

When the people heard of this, they were deeply moved. The bones of Joseph were an explicit reminder of the promises from their childhood. The lyrics of their childhood songs and words of the Scriptures were suddenly coming to life before their eyes; the promises were more than fairy tales passed by elders. God was intentional from the first moment of life on earth, and His intention is true for every one of us.

If you are holding on to a promise that has not yet come to pass, keep holding on. Write the promise out again today, and even again tomorrow. His Word is faithful; His character is true. The route may be different than you expect, and the timing will be all out of sorts from what you'd prefer, but He is the on-time God. In the waiting, He is preparing, developing, and reshaping you to inhabit your promise.

READ EXODUS 13:20-22

> [20] *"After leaving Sukkoth they camped at Etham on the edge of the desert.* [21] *By day the LORD went ahead of them in a pillar of cloud to guide them on their way and by night in a pillar of fire to give them light, so that they could travel by day or night.* [22] *Neither the pillar of cloud by day nor the pillar of fire by night left its place in front of the people."*

Yahweh chose the route. He could be trusted. This pillar of cloud by day and fire by night was a supernatural reminder that He was always present. The children of Israel had not learned to hear the voice of God yet. They needed and relied on a physical representation of the Lord's direction.

Refinement

"The God who is beyond nature has broken into nature and has utilized some of its elements to make it plain that he can deliver people from all the bondages inherent in fallen nature."

All throughout Scripture God uses both fire and clouds to demonstrate Himself:

There are instances in Scripture that mention the significance of clouds. For example, Jesus was received into the clouds in Acts and He will come again with the clouds in Revelation.[6] When Jesus was baptized in Matthew 17, a cloud hovered over Him.

Also, throughout Scripture, you can find stories of God manifesting His will through nature—and especially within fire. Fire itself is a blessing and a danger, even deadly if mishandled or disrespected. It can destroy and purify, yet it also can provide power and comfort. God is in the business of refinement. Just like iron ore, we are in our rawest forms at the start of our journey. We can be useful and serve a purpose, but without the transformative impact of fire and refinement, we cannot become the pillars of strength we are meant to be in this life and in the move of God. The children of Israel needed time to be changed from the inside out to become transformed.

A Prayer

God, teach me how to move this burning fire from a physical representation to the innermost areas of my heart. Show me Your promises and help me to allow Your Word to direct my steps. Your refinement is good, just, and for my benefit. Teach me to trust Your guidance, providence, and Your Word as I approach my next steps. You are revealing Yourself through the biggest and smallest details—I can trust Your strength to sustain and uphold me. Give me patience to wait for Your word, and courage to give You my yes. Amen.

Questions for Reflection

» Is there an area of your life (maybe connected to your promise) that you desire a change, but are afraid of what it will require of you?

» What steps has God asked of you in building trust toward reaching your promise?

» Make a list of times when God showed up strong on your behalf, and then post the list somewhere you will see it daily as a *zakar* of His faithfulness to you.

TUESDAY

Learning to Trust
READ EXODUS 14:1-4

> ¹ "Then the LORD said to Moses, ² 'Tell the Israelites to turn back and encamp near Pi Hahiroth, between Migdol and the sea. They are to be encamped by the sea, directly opposite Baal Zephon. ³ Pharaoh will think, "The Israelites are wandering around the land in confusion, hemmed in by the desert." ⁴ And I will harden Pharaoh's heart, and he will pursue them. But I will gain glory for myself through Pharaoh and all his army, and the Egyptians will know that I am the LORD.' So, the Israelites did this."

The first thing the children of Israel did was to establish a temporary camp after a mostly painless and quick departure from Pharaoh's land. Unfortunately, they packed way too lightly with few supplies, expecting their journey to last only a short while. After all, God asked them to move in haste (12:11). They probably felt a little insecure, but hopeful that the biggest threat (Pharaoh keeping them enslaved) was behind them. Maybe some of them even began to relax! Little did they know, God had designed a divine ruse to demonstrate His ultimate authority to Pharaoh, once and for all.

A look at the context for this part of the story gives us a hint as to the plan itself. What does 14:2–4 say about why God wanted them to make this change in direction?

While God orchestrated this demonstration of His glory, He instructed the Israelites to remember how He guided their ancestors— and He is doing the same for you. It is easy to become swept up in doubt, worry, or frustration when we feel like we've reached a dead end. Instead, let's keep the remembrance of His deliverance for others on the forefront of our minds. He is faithful.

Panic at the Pantheon
READ EXODUS 14:5-9

> [5] "When the king of Egypt was told that the people had fled, Pharaoh and his officials changed their minds about them and said, 'What have we done? We have let the Israelites go and have lost their services!' [6] So he had his chariot made ready and took his army with him. [7] He took six hundred of the best chariots, along with all the other chariots of Egypt, with officers over all of them. [8] The Lord hardened the heart of Pharaoh king of Egypt, so that he pursued the Israelites, who were marching out boldly. [9] The Egyptians—all Pharaoh's horses and chariots, horsemen and troops—pursued the Israelites and overtook them as they camped by the sea near Pi Hahiroth, opposite Baal Zephon."

This part of the study is my absolute favorite. It is easy to read too quickly and miss some very significant parts. Let's dig into this passage a bit. Reread verse 5:

> "When the king of Egypt was told that the people had fled, Pharaoh and his officials changed their minds about them and said, 'What have we done? We have let the Israelites go and have lost their services!'"

"Not only were they expected to build temples and palaces, but they also needed to build military garrisons and store cities for the dramatically enlarged armies. Those kinds of projections required labor forces. It appears the Egyptian people themselves provided the labor for the old kingdoms' pyramids, laboring freely for the distant and unapproachable god-king."[7]

The reality that Egypt just lost most of their workforce hit Pharaoh like the last ton of bricks the Hebrews ever crafted as slaves. The Egyptians were about to face a return to building their temples and cities on their own . . . and that was not what Pharaoh wanted. He wanted a workforce so huge that Egypt's economic prowess would cost them little to nothing. This was a new kingdom with a new Pharaoh who would not be so easily pushed aside.

Pharaoh realized that he sent away the Israelites under his own emotional distress. Between the toll of the plagues and the loss of his son, Pharaoh's decision to command the slaves away was a reaction that caused a ripple effect. The gravity of his decision hit him only after God's people walked away, and he was helpless as Egypt's entire social system threatened to spin out of his control.

I want us to chew on this for a minute and really contextualize this passage to our own escapes from various bondages. This is not a comparison, but an opportunity to engage the story and reflect on our lives. This section really spoke to my own experience with bondage.

I remember the first time I ran from my trafficker. I had started to see through his lies, my scales were falling off, and after a big blow up and a dangerous night on the street, I packed everything and ran. I felt great running. I was done! I was out. The emotional toll helped me over the fear. But as I sat at my aunt's house, my text message alert started beeping. Nothing angry, oh no, quite the contrary. *I miss you. I love you. I promise we won't do it anymore. Just come home. What kind of mother takes their daughter from the only father they've ever known?*

He knew exactly how to manipulate the emotional chase to get me back. And it worked. The truth is, I used to be embarrassed to admit that, until I met many other women who may not relate with being trafficked but have stayed in toxic relationships far too long. Women who left a verbally abusive boyfriend only to have them say they're sorry, but once again their actions do not really change. Women who set boundaries with their toxic family members, but the guilt and shame these relatives continued to spew caused them to cave and compromise those boundaries. Women who have been trapped in financial cycles of either poverty or success, but keep putting up with demeaning, belittling or even harassing bosses because the fear of starting again is terrifying. Either way, I think all of us have moments where we've encountered someone chasing us emotionally, and we've felt stuck at an impasse wondering which way to go.

Both Pharaoh and God Are on the Move
READ EXODUS 14:6-9

> [6] *"So he had his chariot made ready and took his army with him. [7] He took six hundred of the best chariots, along with all the other chariots of Egypt, with officers over all of them. [8] The Lᴏʀᴅ hardened the heart of Pharaoh king of Egypt, so that he pursued the Israelites, who were marching out boldly. [9] The Egyptians—all Pharaoh's horses and chariots, horsemen and troops—pursued the Israelites and overtook them as they camped by the sea near Pi Hahiroth, opposite Baal Zephon."*

Chariots were formidable military weapons in ancient times. A chariot force back then was the equivalent of an Apache helicopter today. It meant business. But why did Pharaoh suddenly think he could win? All his experience with the God of the Israelites proved otherwise. Still, he rallied his troops and wanted to confront the God of the plagues with horses, foot soldiers, and chariots. His pride and belief that he too was a god provided just enough rope to hang himself.[8]

It is important to recognize here that the religion of the Egyptians relied on gods and goddesses who were seen as arbitrary, reactive, and fickle. They changed their minds on a whim to best serve their personal needs and position themselves as the most powerful.[9] Pharaoh was no different; he believed he was a god, and his people agreed—changing his mind made perfect sense to the Egyptians. Little did he know, God was about to show His people His sovereignty so that they could move forward as an army of God.

119

READ EXODUS 14:10-12

> [10] "As Pharaoh approached, the Israelites looked up, and there were the Egyptians, marching after them. They were terrified and cried out to the Lord. [11] They said to Moses, 'Was it because there were no graves in Egypt that you brought us to the desert to die? What have you done to us by bringing us out of Egypt? [12] Didn't we say to you in Egypt, "Leave us alone; let us serve the Egyptians? It would have been better for us to serve the Egyptians than to die in the desert!"'"

It is astounding how quickly the children of Israel forgot about their protection from the plagues! God not only delivered them from the hands of their oppressors, but he protected their drinking water, their livestock, and their firstborn sons! Everything about their lives was owed to God, and they set it aside with accusation at the very first sign of danger.

And yet, their sudden forgetfulness speaks to our behavior as human beings. It makes sense that they might panic at the sight of Egyptian chariots swiftly approaching, flanked by horses and warriors. I know from my work assisting women who escape trafficking that those with a newfound freedom can panic in difficult circumstances, making it hard to focus on the next step. Fear and trauma are real, and they are used by tyrants to control their targets.

The missing characteristic here is trust. How well did the Israelites truly know God? At this point, while they'd had plenty of experiences with Him, had they set their intention to internalize the confidence that He would come through on their behalf? How many Pharaohs throughout their generations of slavery had used, betrayed, or hurt them? Humanity tends to imagine God like we do others in our lives, and it appears the Israelites were no different. There is nothing new under the sun.

Are there characteristics about God that align more with someone from your past than they do the real Yahweh? Are there things about your own situation that make you feel vulnerable and not prepared for the road ahead? Get honest with yourself: Is there a place in your story where you do not yet trust God?

READ EXODUS 14:13-14

> [13] *"Moses answered the people, 'Do not be afraid. Stand firm and you will see the deliverance the LORD will bring you today. The Egyptians you see today you will never see again.* [14] *The LORD will fight for you; you need only to be still.'"*

According to the *NIV Commentary*, what Moses replied to the people was not a word of comfort. We tend to want to picture Braveheart Mel Gibson, throwing his fist in the air with a bellowing "Stand firm!!!" No, no. It is an impatient quip better translated in our culture as, "Just shut up!"[10] He reminds the Israelites that the Lord is fighting for them. I love what Douglas Stuart says about it: "God fights for his people and—no matter how undertrained, ill-equipped, poorly organized or outclassed they might be—he eliminates their foes."[11]

Remember that, beloved, as you face doubt and fear, as your past calls out to you. Surround yourself with people who will call you out, tell you to stop complaining, and encourage you to remember what Yahweh has done.

A Prayer

Holy Spirit, You are good. You are our counselor and guide who brings us into all truth. I thank You that there is nothing new under the sun. You are the same God today who took Your people out of bondage and You are still working miracles among us. I accept that as I tried to escape my iniquity, it was not easy. I accept that my past tried to come after me. But I know that Your plans are to prosper me, not to harm me. And as I trust, pursue, and focus on the promises, I WILL come through victorious, just as did the children of Israel saw with

Pharaoh. Thank you, God, for Your ever-saving power, where I can put my trust. Amen.

Questions for Reflection

» What are you dismissing as a terrible circumstance that could actually be formative to your next season?

» How will your promise move the needle for the generations of your family to come?

» If you are still in the tension of waiting, what confidences or testimonies from your past can you recall to help your faith remain steady?

» Have you ever faced a crossroads and wondered how you were going to get out? What did God do? How can you commemorate this moment?

WEDNESDAY

Building Our Faith Through Action
READ EXODUS 14:21-31

> [21] *"Then Moses stretched out his hand over the sea, and all that night the LORD drove the sea back with a strong east wind and turned it into dry land. The waters were divided, [22] and the Israelites went through the sea on dry ground, with a wall of water on their right and on their left."*

This was not just damp or muddy ground, nor was the Red Sea a shallow, slow-moving creek. The word for "sea" in Hebrew is *yam*. It is not used when referring to swamps or mud flats. This was a wide and deep body of water. Anyone wanting to cross needed a ship and a crew. So when the water parted, the walls of water had to reach nearly fifteen stories high, with dry enough ground to taunt and tempt the Egyptians into a pursuit. No sensible chariot commander would have taken the chance otherwise.

Moses's staff in the air was a signal and reminder of the covering God offered through the plagues. And suddenly, the children of Israel understood. They were moving forward, and this was not the moment for hesitation or fear. Even the length of time it would take for them to cross the dry ground would take hours, and maybe they couldn't even see the shore on the other side. But sometimes we have to move forward even when the future is unclear or the waters look too choppy. How much confidence would you have walking alongside those intimidating waters? Yet just like the Israelites, our future is secure when we are following God. We can trust Him to be our protector. He will not only lead us, but He will protect us along the way.

Available for Service

The real nugget here is often overlooked. GOD USES PEOPLE. John Oswalt breaks it down so clearly:

"God regularly works through human agency. Moses raised his hand and the sea parted. Moses raised his hand and the water rushed back. But Moses acted on the command of God; it was God who did the work. The agent does not perform the work without the power and direction of God, but God does not accomplish his purposes except through the human agent."[12]

I find it encouraging to know that God wants to use you and me to accomplish His plans. When I meditate on the fact that I am included in the intricate details of God's heart for the world, I get excited! I dream about the different ways God can use my story or my hands and feet to shift the world around me toward the kingdom of heaven. Do you ever consider your role? What are some ways that God can partner with you?

READ EXODUS 14:23-31

[23] "The Egyptians pursued them, and all Pharaoh's horses and chariots and horsemen followed them into the sea. [24] During the last watch of the night the LORD looked down from the pillars of fire and cloud at the Egyptian army and threw it into confusion. [25] He jammed the wheels of their chariots so that they had difficulty driving. And the Egyptians said, 'Let's get away from the Israelites! The LORD is fighting for them against Egypt.'

[26] "Then the LORD said to Moses, 'Stretch out your hand over the sea so that the waters may flow back over the Egyptians and their chariots and horsemen.' [27] Moses stretched out his hand over the sea, and at daybreak the sea went back to its place. The Egyptians were fleeing toward it, and the LORD swept them into the sea. [28] The water flowed back and covered the chariots and horsemen—the entire army of Pharaoh that had followed the Israelites into the sea. Not one of them survived.

[29] "But the Israelites went through the sea on dry ground, with a wall of water on their right and on their left. [30] That day the LORD saved Israel from the hands of the Egyptians, and Israel saw the Egyptians lying dead on the shore. [31] And when the Israelites saw the mighty hand of the LORD displayed against the Egyptians, the people feared the LORD and put their trust in him and in Moses his servant."

I don't know about you, but there is something so refreshing about God's vengeance—is that okay to say? It was the chariots that the Israelites feared, and yet the chariots became the literal vehicle ending the pursuit of their enemies. Once again, God showed the Egyptians that their king was no match for Yahweh. Even though the children of Israel had a long and arduous journey ahead of them, the first part was done. They were truly free from the Egyptians. Regardless of the trouble they might encounter along the rest of their travels, they could rest assured that "the end is always in God's sight and His plan will not be thwarted."[13]

One thing we all know for certain, experiences can build our faith: If we position our hearts in a posture of hopeful expectation, we will keep our eyes above the waves. There is no question in my mind that upon witnessing the bodies of their pursuers, the Israelites fell in awe of this great miracle. In the middle of our suddenly-dry Red Sea floor, we can choose to put one foot in front of the next and keep walking . . . or we can choose to retreat. God is the great Redeemer; He is always in the mood to renovate our storylines and deepen our roots of confidence in His character.

God Comes to Us

God continually used physical representations because the Israelites had not yet learned to hear His voice. He also used the physical representations from their leader Moses, when in Exodus 14:16 and 14:26 Moses raised his hands over the sea. What did this symbolize to the Hebrews at the time? They recognized that God was speaking to their circumstances by moving Moses into action. They saw the move of God manifesting right in their neediest moment.

God speaks to us right where we are. In ancient Eastern thought, deities controlled war, the weather, and were a part of the everyday lives of the people. God parted the Red Sea not just to rescue His people but to speak their language. We see this in the New Testament when Greeks and Gentiles converted to Christianity. The message of Jesus being the Son of God was an easy transitional thought since they previously worshiped Greek mythology.

Find an index card (or a paper about the same size), write down the largest faith-building experience you have had, and put it somewhere near at hand (you could even turn it into a bookmark!). The next time you face trouble, pull out this card and remind yourself that this experience changed your mind once; allow it to continue to change your perspective when the waters before you seem too deep to cross.

A Prayer

God, give me a breath of fresh air. You have used so many moments—great and mundane—to speak to me in a way I will understand. Help me to see the towering waters around me and to step with faith that You will dry the ground beneath my feet. I can't see the other side, but You can. You are the staff raised above me and the crowd of support following me through the wilderness. Thank You for giving me a greater level of confidence that in You, I am secure. Amen.

Questions for Reflection

» How did God build the faith of the Hebrews through this miracle of parting the sea?

» When was the last time you recall God encountering your life and moving physically through the life of another to demonstrate His love and rescue for you?

» How has God relied on you as a human agent, a copartner, in His plan for someone else?

THURSDAY

When the Fear Fades

I love gospel music. I got saved at the age of twenty-one, and it was a time in my life when I had to constantly lean on God for deliverance and comfort. I would crank up and worship with all of my heart, singing along with artists like CeCe Winans and Erica and Tina Campbell from Mary Mary at the top of my lungs. To this day, I can put on Shekinah Glory Ministry, and I feel immediately in the presence of the Lord.

There are seasons of life that require songs of lament, and some that call for celebration. Throughout the ages, God has used music to comfort and encourage His people.

Today's verse is found in Exodus 15:1–21, also known as "The Song of Moses and Miriam."

Take just a few minutes to read the celebration that the Israelites sang about God; read it out loud if you can. Let the words wash over you now that you know the weight and gravity that the children of Israel were coming out of. After generations of enslavement, the moment of victory over their captors became the stage for Moses to declare the goodness, strength, and glory of God.

Israel's faith was growing, and it's worth noting. They had seen horrible plagues ravage the Egyptians and not touch them. They listened to the grief-stricken wails of their captors echo through the night after the angel of death passed over their own doorways. They watched towering walls of water stand at attention as they crossed the Red Sea on dry ground. God was leading them, step by step, where He wanted them to go, teaching them along the way.

Without reading through these stories in Exodus, we might quickly dismiss the details and people of the Old Testament Bible stories as simple characters. It might be easy to write them off as fickle failures. After all, this is the same group of people who would eventually wander the desert for another 40 years before entering the promised land. But when we engage Scriptures in the context they were written, we are invited into the bigger picture. These were human beings. Beautifully complex, intricate, and sometimes confused people—just like us.

I know I'm not alone when I look at the response of the Hebrews over the last few chapters and realize that I, too, have had life-altering, faith-building encounters. When God invited me back to the United States after fleeing to London, it was His hand that made the way for my return. I learned so much more about leaning into His faithfulness simply because I had no other choice. It was time to leave behind my fear and watch God fulfill His words at my side.

It takes receiving a victory over a storm to grow our faith. But when was the last time God orchestrated something on your behalf without your engagement? It happens, of course. But He is far more interested in the partnership—the active relationship—with the ones He loves. Obviously, we don't want to experience storms. Humans are programmed to keep themselves as safe and secure as possible; to accept and even desire the uncomfortable known circumstance over the potentially better but unknown. But if we want to see our faith develop from fearful captives to the empowered, confident, and trusting children of God, then we must decide when we are going to take the next step onto the dry sea floor. Trials form our character into the people we want to become. Through the song of Moses, we hear the awe of the Hebrews at the actions of the Lord.

They had just crossed over and escaped a watery grave. They had watched their mighty enemy sink under a towering mountain of crashing waves. They now stood on the other side, coming to the full realization that God had decisively destroyed the enemy and ended the Israelites season of slavery.

We need to live in these moments of victory. To remember the stories of Scripture, and to remember they were humans like us. It is our high calling to posture our hearts and position our thoughts to dwell on these miracles. I think the best way to do this is to recognize the characteristics of God that resonate the deepest with the cry of our hearts. Are we people who rejoice the loudest at orphans finding homes? Then the justice of God to make families out of the lonely will bring us great joy. Maybe we want to see the hopeless healed of their addictions. The restorative heart of God is to be greatly celebrated as He rearranges the priorities and inner workings of our hearts, minds, and lives.

If you are in a season of breaking through fear or simply need a reminder of the miracles He has worked in your life, take a moment to read chapter 15 again. Identify the characteristics of God that embody the attributes of what and who He is to you right now. Have you experienced His provision? Remember it well; it will break the fear of lack when you again find yourself in great need.

When the Trust Fades

But as we know, this passionate "in the moment" trust faded for the Israelites. It reminds me of the same lie that the enemy came and whispered to Eve in the creation story.

"Are God's intentions toward us really good? Or, as the snake said in the garden, is God, like everyone else, looking out for their own interests and quite willing to use or abuse his creatures for those interests?"[14]

Have you ever felt like this? Is there anything happening in your life right now that is leading to this kind of processing in your mind? Freedom is waiting if we can leave behind and repent of that type of thinking.

We must remind ourselves that God's promises are true. He always comes through, even when we can't see immediate results. Does that mean we are going to experience peace through all aspects of our challenges? Of course not. We are not naïve; we are in fact deepening the wells of our wisdom. We are engaging in a reconciliation between our anxieties and our hopes. The path set before us is not always easy or quick, but we can trust that the path we are traveling is within the will of God to prepare us for our next adventure: occupying our promised land.

If you find yourself struggling with the idea of reconciling your fears as valid and still remaining open to trusting God, I want to relieve a little pressure. Remember: Even Moses pushed back with excuses and fears to the call of God. The way we can engage our hearts and the heart of God is through prayer. Prayer that recognizes God is faithful; that enters into His heart with gratitude and into His love with awe and praise. When you recenter your thoughts on your God instead of your habit of catastrophizing (overthinking about worst-case scenarios), your faith is stirred into confidence one word at a time.

A Prayer

Lord, thank You that I can trust You. You are the God of the Israelites, faithfully leading them through their captivity. I am sorry for doubting Your ways, Your tactics, and Your intentions. You are a God of strategy and fulfillment. Please forgive me for my murmuring, my questioning, and my complaining. You are faithful to make Your affections for me as plain as a cloud in the day and a fire at night. Keep my eyes locked on You as I continue walking on this unknown path toward my promised land. I trust You and I am allowing my trust to deepen every day. Amen!

Questions for Reflection

» In the Song of Moses, how is God portrayed?

» Think of a time when your trust suddenly exploded at God's faithfulness. Do you still have that same "level" of confidence in His provision today? What changed?

» How can you engage God's trust without dismissing your real concerns or fears? Minimizing our anxieties is not the way to trust in God. Acknowledging His provision and remembering the truth of how He comes through on our behalf, to His glory, is what stirs our hearts to trust and builds our confidence. Write a prayer of your own, expressing your gratitude and awe at the truth of what God has done in your life until now. Let those memories carry you into the next steps you must take.

FRIDAY

The Posture of Our Hearts
READ EXODUS 15:22-17:7

I was walking to an event in Berlin with a good friend and doctor in psychology. We had been sharing a room at a local hotel and as we walked and talked, she said something that caused me to get a bit prickly. I stiffened and grew shorter in our exchanges. My mind raced to possible scenarios happening behind my back as insecurity crept its way into my heart. We reached our destination and put our things down at our seats. She stopped me and asked, "What I said back there—did I hurt your feelings or trigger you?"

Tears welled up in my eyes.

"I don't know if I can tell the difference."

Trauma had done that. It had caused me to be unsure when something was causing a visceral response that needed healing and therapy or a regular emotional response to my feelings being hurt over something that caused insecurity, rejection, or uncertainty.

When today's passage begins, it is exactly one month after the Red

Sea crossing. In the one month since the Israelites have been wandering, they have been experiencing their first taste of freedom, finally outside the influence of Egyptian control.

Four major moments occurred during this time, recorded in chapters 15, 16, and 17. First, Moses threw wood into a spring of bitter water, and it was made sweet so the people could drink it. Then, God brought quail and manna to feed them. Third was an instance when Moses struck a rock and fresh water poured out. We will look at each of these moments and how God was working to address and impact the mindset of the Israelites.

The Israelites continued to complain against Moses and God. When they grew thirsty, they didn't simply ask for water; they complained that Moses had brought them all the way out into the desert to die. And when they were hungry, they told Moses that in Egypt they sat around and ate pots of meat, but now they would starve. This was untrue, of course. But still the Israelites cycled through complaint after complaint, even to the point of wanting to stone Moses.

Present discomfort and past security can make us grow weary of the unknown path ahead. We are tempted to focus on the past instead of the future promises. And when we are caught up romanticizing what we had and lost, we forget to posture our hearts in a position of praise.

READ WHAT GOD SAYS TO THE CHILDREN OF ISRAEL IN 15:25-26

> [25] "And he cried to the Lord, and the Lord showed him a log, and he threw it into the water, and the water became sweet.
>
> "There the Lord made for them a statute and a rule, and there he tested them, [26] saying, 'If you will diligently listen to the voice of the Lord your God, and do that which is right in his eyes, and give ear to his commandments and keep all his statutes, I will put none of the diseases on you that I put on the Egyptians, for I am the Lord, your healer.'" (ESV)

Why do you think the author is emphasizing the testing of the people? God had shown them His care, His provision, His protection, and His desire for relationship. Now, it was time for them to put their faith, trust, and belief into action.

Whatever You Practice Becomes Stronger

Whatever we give our attention to becomes the focal point of our lives. Whatever we choose to practice gets stronger. You can choose to practice kindness or gossip. You get that choice, dear sister, and if you choose God's way, He will continue to put you in situations allowing you to choose obedience. But He is a good Father and a great teacher, so whenever you fail that test, He'll let you take it over and over again, just like the children of Israel.

You are the one who guards your emotional health. How much time do you spend scrolling on your phone versus building into your physical or emotional health or your family and community? No one holds the key to unlocking your joy, your character, or your time—except for you. We must remain aware of the quality of our thought lives. It is often the storms and trials in life that will absolutely stir up the dredges from the bottom of our hearts.

The children of Israel found themselves in test after test. They had a choice to engage with the conflict internally and rework the character to trust and believe, or to remain stubborn and bitter at their difficulties.

Following Direction

In Exodus 16:3–35, we read about two more miracles of provision.

> 16:3 *"and the people of Israel said to them, 'Would that we had died by the hand of the LORD in the land of Egypt, when we sat by the meat pots and ate bread to the full, for you have brought us out into this wilderness to kill this whole assembly with hunger.'" (ESV)*

This statement by the Israelites is untrue. Had they remembered things inaccurately? Isn't it interesting how our brains work? Often, we can distort reality. We know that due to refrigeration it was very rare to have meat to eat in Egypt and even less likely for slaves to have access to it. Diets consisted of rough bread full of rocks that broke everyone's teeth as well as figs and dates.

» What did the children cry out for in 16:3? _____ and _____.
» What does God deliver in 16:8? _____ and _____.

We can't forget to look between verse 3 and 8 to see the very specific instructions the Lord gave the children for the collection of manna. Only enough for the day itself—but some couldn't resist gathering more.

Chapter 16:12–28 gives us a great reminder of how God provided, gave clear directions, tested them, and allowed them to try again.

Take account of what happened in the following verses:

» 16:12

» 16:13

» 16:20

» 16:22

» 16:27–28

What do you think God was trying to teach them?

Even the apostle Paul references Exodus 16:18 in his second letter to the Corinthians. When the Hebrews were gathering manna, some gathered extra and some, not quite enough. Paul reminds us that because of God's faithfulness there is provision enough for the day—as long as we remain in line with the generosity of God. Getting stuck in a poverty mentality robs us from the generosity of God, loses the lesson of HIS provision, and ends up allowing pride to rely on ourselves to creep in.

Not only is this a lesson for all of us, but it was especially important for a group of people who needed to learn how to rely on Yahweh if they were going to be successful warriors in taking over the promised land.

A Faith That Grows

As we watch God provide and move in our lives, our faith can grow.

I love the story of Peter walking on the water because there is so much richness that we initially overlook. What many of us fail to remember is that Peter had lived and remained faithful through TWO massive storms, not just this one. During the first storm (Matt. 8:23–27), Jesus was in the boat with Peter and the other apostles. He awoke from a nap to chaos and His disciples afraid. Jesus calmed the sea by simply speaking to the storm. Peter's faith grew immensely in that moment! So much so that during the second storm (Matt. 14:22–33), Peter believed strongly enough in the words of Jesus to get out, step over the edge, and walk on the water too!

Living through one storm can strengthen our faith for the second. We need these experiences to grow and build our confidence in Him.

So, what is the key to moving through the storm? Praise and worship. The key is keeping our hearts in a posture of praise through every flash of lightning and crash of thunder. Not murmuring and complaining; not bucking, kicking, or fighting. Of course, we must give ourselves time to grieve the loss of our ideals. Our "must be nice" responses when others seem to have an easier time are valid and deserve a chance to breathe. But as we are learning to dream again, we can learn to shelve our cynicism and dream with God for a more hopeful future. This is when our worship becomes our weapon. This is where we grow.

The Israelites knew that God *could* come through, but did He *want* to and *would* He? Time and again, they lacked trust and struggled to keep their hopes alive. If only we could learn the truth about His faithfulness from a single storm. But like the Israelites, we have to build the habit of stirring our memories every time a storm comes.

We see their response in the fourth miracle in Exodus 17:1–7.

Write a few notes about:

» 17:3

» 17:6

» 17:7

Like us, the children of Israel had highs and lows. One day, they marched across a dry seabed, leaving the only enemy they'd ever known behind, and then next they were dying of thirst in an unending desert, with no end in sight. They had not truly released their grip on the past. The children of Israel needed to change the channel of their minds to anticipation and hope, based on their experiences. Instead, they chose to grumble and dismiss God's guidance. In the waiting, they did not stand up to praise God in the midst of the uncertainty. Instead, they walked in circles for forty years.

And still, through the wilderness, God was continuing to build character so that they'd be ready to step into their destiny.

Exodus literally means "a way out" or "a departure." We end this week's devotional with that happening. The children of Israel were transformed from Hebrews to Israelites. They became a people set apart, leaving captivity with the riches plundered from Egypt. They received physical representations of fire and clouds as visual promises that God was with them. They followed a leader who showed he was actively partnering with the Lord. They were rescued from violent destruction at the Red Sea, their enemies overtaken by the deity who controlled the land and sea: Yahweh. And now, the Israelites were wandering free, on their way to the promised land. This could be where the story ended as far as

God's lessons for their growth as a people. But just like when you realize the climax of the movie still has 45 minutes left for resolution, there is more to come from God to Moses and the Israelites. Which means there is still so much more that we can glean from their journey as well.

A Prayer

God, I know You're in this storm with me and near me. I trust that You are faithful to complete the good work in my life that You have started. In Hebrews 11:1, we remember that faith is the substance of things hoped for and the evidence of things not seen. This is more than just praying for the rent check to come in. This is about my character along the way, because that is what I need in the seasons to come. I want to reach my promises, God, and I know that I need to strengthen certain things in me to do so. Faithfulness, long suffering, patience, kindness . . . I will not be found remaining on the sidelines, waiting for Your long arm of rescue. I will be found in my own story, faithful and active. I will break boundaries and expectations with my own expectation that I am going to encounter storms along the way. And when they arrive, I will be found singing of Your glory, Your affection, and Your kindness. In the waiting, I am learning to trust You as worthy of my praise. Amen.

Questions for Reflection

» What attitudes lay behind all the complaints of the Israelites?

» Where in your life are you experiencing discomfort with an unknown outcome? Check your heart: Are you recalling a position of confidence and praise toward the Lord, or are you somewhere between grumbling Israelite and resistant Moses?

» Heart check: Are you more focused on the past or your future? Are you grumbling and doubting or praising and practicing? How can you take the children of Israel's example to heart?

» What does the Word remind us of being tested? (See James 1:2–4; 1 Peter 4:12–13.)

» What are you putting your trust in? (See Rom. 5:1–5; Prov. 3:5.)

» What does God have planned for you and me? (See Phil. 1:6; Rom. 8:28.)

REMEMBERING YOUR WHY

THIS WEEK we are going to explore specific sections of Exodus 17:1–35. Feel free to read it all, of course, but we will examine various passages each day for a high-level view.

Have you ever started a new career or moved to a new city? It can be exciting and overwhelming all at the same time. The new adventure is on the horizon with loads of possibilities but also the little things that can be forgotten. Where is a new favorite coffee shop or where do I get my hair done? I know, first-world problems. But there is an expectation of showing up at that new office or that new church and things falling into place easily.

What about things that aren't so exciting? A job loss, a divorce, leaving a hard season and starting over can be overwhelming too, in a scary and painful way.

I have started over with nothing.

Running for my life was the hardest, scariest decision I've ever made. Because you're leaving with nothing. You have no social capital, no education. Not even a pillow or fork to your name. I slept on couches and got on food stamps. Getting "rescued" wasn't what I imagined. I had escaped on my own, yes, but I know I had a huge gap in job history, a criminal record, and a ton of PTSD. I was put right back to the same vulnerabilities that led to trafficking in the first place.

I remember thinking, *Now what? Now what am I going to do with the rest of my life?*

One night I sat at my kitchen table and got mad at God. *Is this really what You saved me for? Is this the abundant life that the church talks about? I don't want this either.*

God replied, *If you give Me the same amount of time you gave the enemy, I'll never be outdone.*

Things got radically better, though it wasn't easy. Turning your life around is hard. It's tough to dig your heels in and navigate this new world that you know nothing about when you want to go back to what's familiar. It's determining in your heart that you will do the opposite of what your brain is telling you to do. It's strengthening your spirit man and saying no to your flesh. Its understanding that neurology and trauma are real and working deliberately to take thoughts captive until they form new pathways in Christ.

It's having a "come to Jesus" moment with yourself and recognize that some new habits, new behaviors, and new structure will be necessary to move you into your NEXT.

The Hebrews also may have been expecting to transition immediately into their promise and take possession of their new land and freedom. They had lived under Egyptian law for hundreds of years. Every decision was dictated, every choice made for them. How could they possibly move into a new land, protect themselves from invaders, and begin to build a new kingdom? They couldn't. Not yet. They just weren't ready, and I'm sure at the moment they couldn't see it.

After all, they had made a dramatic exit from Egypt with Pharaoh hot on their heels. They witnessed miraculous walls of water standing at attention as they crossed the Red Sea on a dry riverbed. They had been given manna and water from rocks. They knew He was able. And now they were walking in circles, camping like nomads without any military training to protect themselves from invaders who had heard that the Israelites had all of Egypt's gold. They were waiting to move into Canaan, to take it over, and God said *wait!* They had seen the miracle deliverance from Pharoah. Why wouldn't God deliver them into the land of milk and honey with the same flair?

God knew they weren't ready. He said that He was not able to bring "these stiff-necked people" into the promised land because they were not learning the lessons they needed to learn. They had not developed the strength, the tenacity, faith, or skill sets needed to move forward.

And so, two million Israelite people began to settle in camps on Mount Sinai to wait for a word from the Lord. I can imagine the thoughts and questions they must have had right away as God told them to pause indefinitely in order to prepare them and teach them the lessons they would need to know before they continued.

It's hard to be in transition, isn't it? Sometimes God calls us to a long season of waiting while He prepares us for what's next. It can be exhausting. We face burnout, discouragement, and disappointment. But we are called to keep going. Just like the Hebrews, if we can learn to trust Him and hear His voice, He will lead the way.

MONDAY

I was about to go on maternity leave with our second daughter, Ila. I was a full eight months pregnant and as a newly married couple we had been saving up for these twelve weeks with no work. For the last year we had been paying only $500 in rent per month as a caretaking agreement for my boss. Their house had been on the market while they moved out of state, and Matt and I were taking care of it while agents brought through potential buyers.

Suddenly, what felt like out of nowhere the house sold and we were given thirty days to move out. What was worse was that my due date fell on the exact move-out date. Once again, I was upset with God. *Really Lord? You couldn't have waited 30 days or even done this 30 days sooner?*

Begrudgingly, we packed our home into a storage unit and slept on a mattress on the floor with the hospital bag by the door ready to go. Our plan was to sleep at my grandma's until we could find another place.

I mean, rent anywhere for a family of four would never be $500, not to mention paying the first and last month's rent required to get into another rental would have taken every bit of what we had been saving for maternity leave. I felt discouraged and defeated and, let's be honest, hormonal.

My boss flew into town to sign the paperwork and asked if he could come by. We agreed, of course, and he got there and looked around at the empty house and said matter of factly but with a smile on his face, "Well, the buyers have pulled out and we'd like you to stay." I was a bit perturbed. I swept my arm around to display the emptiness he clearly didn't see and responded, "We've already paid for everything to go into storage."

He responded, "We'll lower your rent by $200 if you stay." I almost started crying. Right then I felt the Lord whisper, *You've been praying for maternity leave. and I just lowered your bills by $200. Next time stop murmuring and complaining and praise Me through the storm.*

We pick up today's reading having watched some incredible miracles as well as the children of Israel's struggle to learn lessons in the process. We learned about the context of Egypt, which gives us more understanding of Moses and the people's mindset going in. They watched God keep them safe from the plagues, part the Red Sea, and move them closer and closer toward their promises.

Write down the places you see in these verses:

» Ex. 15:27

» Ex. 16:1

» Ex. 16:35

» Ex. 17:1

» Ex. 17:8

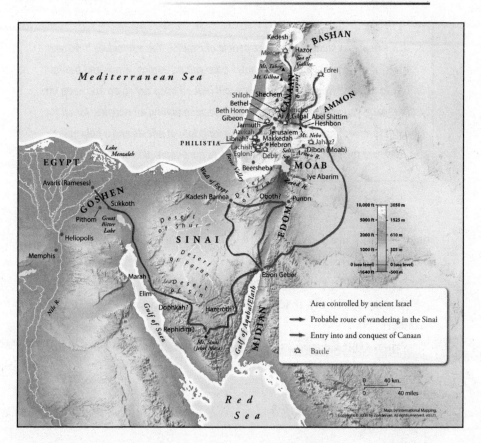

We will get back to the timeline in next week's lesson, but I want us to get an idea in this lesson of the journey that the children of Israel were on.

READ EXODUS 19:1-6 (ESV)

[1] "On the third new moon after the people of Israel had gone out of the land of Egypt, on that day they came into the wilderness of Sinai. [2] They set out from Rephidim and came into the wilderness of Sinai, and they encamped in the wilderness. There Israel encamped before the mountain, [3] while Moses went up to God. The Lord called to him out of the mountain, saying, 'Thus you shall say

> *to the house of Jacob, and tell the people of Israel:* ⁴ *"You yourselves have seen what I did to the Egyptians, and how I bore you on eagles' wings and brought you to myself.* ⁵ *Now therefore, if you will indeed obey my voice and keep my covenant, you shall be my treasured possession among all peoples, for all the earth is mine;* ⁶ *and you shall be to me a kingdom of priests and a holy nation." 'These are the words that you shall speak to the people of Israel.'"*

In Exodus 33:1–2 we see the Lord give another command to depart and go further north. Nearly forty years they have been camping, settling, packing up, and sending men to the next city to check it out. (See Num. 13:26; Deut. 1:19.) Ever led by the pillar of cloud and pillar of fire.

(You can actually read their entire mapped journey documented in Numbers 33.)

When God asks you to wait, will you wait? When He asks you to move, will you move?

READ DEUTERONOMY 2:7-8

How many years did it take the Israelites to get from slavery to their promise?

Much physical preparation and spiritual preparation was necessary. It was going to take a people who heard the voice of the Lord and obeyed. They had to trust Him, rely on Him, and believe what He was telling them to be true.

Let's also not forget that these people had plunder from Egypt. Here you have this nomadic group with no land, no fortified city with walls to protect them, no military experience or training. They wanted one. They were being called to one. To become a nation, but they weren't one yet.

There have been many times in my life where I have felt nomadic. I have packed up a couple suitcases or boxes and am sleeping at a friend's or family's until the next thing opens up. I feel unsettled and restless and the more time that goes by I wonder if I heard from God right. *Did I get enough confirmations?* Why wasn't a door opening for the next thing? *Are you there, God?* I am sure the children of Israel felt this way for forty years. You would think one would give up hope in that time, and maybe this is a good indicator/reminder of how they responded to these in-betweens. It allows us to check our hearts.

A Prayer

Lord, thank You that Your plans for us are to prosper us and to give us hope for a future. We know our feelings can change all the time and quickly. Thank You that we do not walk by feelings but hold on to You and Your truth to be our guide. Help us to hear You better, to be obedient to Your leadership and guidance. Let us not be one step ahead or behind the place You have for us each day. Amen.

Questions for Reflection

» Have you had a time when it took longer to move into the next season than you had hoped?

» How did you position your heart during that time? Do you have ideas of what you can do better next time?

» What are some ways to remind yourself to check your heart when feelings arise that may not align with all that God has for you?

TUESDAY

Checking the Boxes
READ EXODUS 17:7-16

The Western vision of an American retirement plan romanticizes a land flowing with milk and honey. As Americans, we claim it as our own inheritance, imagining an empty, clear plot of land on which to build our dream home and relax into a life of simplicity and rest. It's an easy "check the box" type of path, right? Just work your to-do list and things will fall into place. I wonder if the Hebrews thought that all they had to do was "check the boxes" and they would stroll right in and make themselves at home in the promised land.

Before we become too comfortable and starry-eyed, let's go back to chapter 13:5:

> *"When the Lord brings you into the land of the Canaanites, Hittites, Amorites, Hivites and Jebusites . . ."*

That's right, there were already other people living in the land promised to the Israelites. There were nations of people who had fought and settled there, and who were willing to fight to stay there. They weren't just going to move out because the Israelites told them God had promised it to them.

A Call to Conquer

In order to occupy the promised land, the Israelites had to recognize that their promise of becoming their own nation included actually doing some serious work. This was no small task. They would need to work on themselves, their character, and their trust in God to step out in faith. They needed to learn to hear God's voice, because they were going to war! Their promise was not to inherit an uninhabited land that required no battles. It was time to fight for what they wanted. Even though they had been slowly strengthening their trust and reliance on him, it wasn't yet enough.

Standing Strong

Israel's battle with the Amalekites gives us a good picture of what it means to pull together for a common purpose and also a reminder that they faced constant attack for their Egyptian plunder.

READ EXODUS 17:8-16

> [8] *"The Amalekites came and attacked the Israelites at Rephidim.* [9] *Moses said to Joshua, 'Choose some of our men and go out to fight the Amalekites. Tomorrow I will stand on top of the hill with the staff of God in my hands.'*
>
> [10] *"So Joshua fought the Amalekites as Moses had ordered, and Moses, Aaron and Hur went to the top of the hill.* [11] *As long as Moses held up his hands, the Israelites were winning, but whenever he lowered his hands, the Amalekites were winning.* [12] *When Moses' hands grew tired, they took a stone and put it under him and he sat on it. Aaron and Hur held his hands up—one on one side, one on the other—so that his hands remained steady till sunset.* [13] *So Joshua overcame the Amalekite army with the sword.*
>
> [14] *"Then the* Lord *said to Moses, 'Write this on a scroll as something to be remembered and make sure that Joshua hears it, because I will completely blot out the name of Amalek from under heaven.'*
>
> [15] *"Moses built an altar and called it The* Lord *is my Banner.* [16] *He said, 'Because hands were lifted up against the throne of the* Lord, *the* Lord *will be at war against the Amalekites from generation to generation.'"*

What a picture! Joshua was fighting alongside his troops, but he could not have been victorious without Moses lifting his hands. Moses could not continue without Aaron and Hur by his side. Every person played a part, and every person was crucial to the victory. Like a clock, every cog works at a different pace, but if they are out of sync, the clock stops. We must work like Moses, Joshua, Aaron and Hur, appreciating and encouraging one another. Be the first person to stand in line to cheer another friend on. Don't let discouragement take root in your heart and grow into bitterness and resentment.

You may not always be called into physical battle, yet you are absolutely in a spiritual battle. How you choose to fight your ungodly thoughts will determine your character.

I was working one afternoon when I received a call from a donor telling me that a lady from another organization had badmouthed me to get us cut from funding. I had had difficult interactions with this group in the past as they seemed to despise faith-based groups. I took the call and hung up angry. I started playing scenarios in mind of what I would say to her! *Enough was enough. You've crossed the line. You have a problem with me? You forget that I'll fight you?!* It played in my head like a bad movie scene. Suddenly, Numbers 23 popped into my head. *Not now, Lord.*

I caved and opened my Bible and these words popped out at me:

> [8] *"How can I curse those whom God has not cursed?"*

How can I denounce whom the Lord has not denounced?

> [11] *"And Balak said to Balaam, 'What have you done to me? I took you to curse my enemies, and behold, you have done nothing but bless them.'* [12] *And he answered and said, 'Must I not take care to speak what the Lord puts in my mouth?'"* (ESV)

So, I chose to fight differently. Instead of calling her, I stood by my office window and started speaking blessings over her: funding so prosperous she wouldn't need to seek others, favor and purpose that would keep her so fulfilled and busy that she wouldn't have time to worry about what others were doing, strong believers around her to remind her of her goodness. And as I warred in the Spirit for her, something changed in me.

Have you ever stood by anyone who was fighting an exhausting fight? Have you ever had anyone hold you up when you felt like you couldn't go on? Friend, we weren't made to do this life alone. We were meant for community. And when we experience strength on every side, or when we watch someone fight with everything they have, we are changed and strengthened.

A Prayer

Father, help me to remember that although You see the big picture, You also have the best intentions for my life. Strengthen my mind and heart for the battles You've called me to; teach me when I need to rest. Help me to play the part You have for me and to help others when they grow weary. May I always choose Your will over my own comfort, and may I follow You around every twist and turn in the path.

Questions for Reflection

» In your own words, what was the meaning of the altar Moses built in response to Israel's battle? (See 17:15.)

» Have you had to choose a different response than usual in your life?

>> What came out of that for you personally?

>> What does God want to strengthen in you right now?

WEDNESDAY

Fighting Burnout
READ EXODUS 18:1-27

Can you imagine it? The Hebrew people had made an exhausting trek to Mount Sinai carrying all the plunder from Egypt, and now they were crowded in camps, waiting for God to tell them what to do next. Two million people living in close quarters with one another, storing the wealth from Egypt in their tents, and if they hadn't already, they began to question if they had made the right choice to follow Moses. They quarreled, they sweated, they grew weary, they were angry and hungry—or hangry.

To make things worse, up to this point, they have lived a life of slavery, without any type of military strength or training or weapons. Now, they were surrounded by less-than-friendly neighboring nations on all sides. They were not only in dangerous territory, but they were in a dangerous situation.

But the enemy surrounding them was not the only thing they had to worry about. There was also trouble among neighbors and even within families in the camps. While Joshua was helping keep away the other nations who were trying to take the plunder, Moses was tending to the people, and it was a huge job. Not only were families faced with tending their children and everyday responsibilities, but they also had to take care of any other needs you can imagine in a "tent city." There began to be issues with boundaries inside the camps. The Hebrews began spending so much time back-biting and arguing, eventually over time Moses spent his days, from sunup until sundown, fielding complaints and settling disputes. Needless to say, Moses began burning out.

Moses's temper, which we already knew was bad from his younger years, may have begun to subside with wisdom and age, but Scripture tells us that he was basically annoyed, frustrated, and angry with God over the Hebrews and their attitudes toward one another. No moms can relate to this feeling, I'm sure (insert sarcasm).

What does 18:24 tell us about Moses's character?

We know from Moses's childhood that his heart for justice and fairness was extreme. Even though he was called to be a leader during this difficult time in the history of the Hebrews, we also see the danger of leadership burnout.

Apparently, Moses was not dealing with the stress very well, and we can see from previous chapters that his frustrations had been building:

READ EXODUS 15:24-26

²⁴ "So the people grumbled against Moses, saying, 'What are we to drink?' ²⁵ Then Moses cried out to the LORD, and the LORD showed him a piece of wood. He threw it into the water, and the water became fit to drink. There the LORD issued a ruling and instruction for them and put them to the test. ²⁶ He said, 'If you listen carefully to the LORD your God and do what is right in his eyes, if you pay attention to his commands and keep all his decrees, I will not bring on you any of the diseases I brought on the Egyptians, for I am the LORD, who heals you.'"

READ EXODUS 16:6-7

> ^{6} "So Moses and Aaron said to all the Israelites, 'In the evening you will know that it was the Lord who brought you out of Egypt, ^{7} and in the morning, you will see the glory of the Lord, because he has heard your grumbling against him. Who are we, that you should grumble against us?'"

READ EXODUS 17:2-3

> ^{2} "So they quarreled with Moses and said, 'Give us water to drink.'
>
> "Moses replied, 'Why do you quarrel with me? Why do you put the Lord to the test?'"
>
> ^{3} "But the people were thirsty for water there, and they grumbled against Moses. They said, 'Why did you bring us up out of Egypt to make us and our children and livestock die of thirst?'"

Pretty tense, right? It also seems that Moses couldn't spare a minute to tend to his own family. To make matters even worse, Moses faced trouble in his own tent, and the Bible even tells us that his wife and their two sons went back home to Midian. I mean, we already knew something was brewing when she called him a bridegroom of blood for wanting to circumcise his sons, but now Moses's lack of margin for family life was taking a real strain on the household.

I have learned that sometimes frustration, burnout, and a lack of direction can bleed into other areas of our lives. Have you ever found that to be true? Moses certainly lived through it in this part of the story. Working 24/7 long enough can cause a person to implode.

Even though this new nation of people didn't see the lack of sustainability, God did. Their leader was alone and overwhelmed. They were fighting with each other with no end in sight. There was no forward movement, and they couldn't go back. They were stuck.

I love this scene when Zipporah and the boys returned home to her father. I picture Jethro not even letting them drop their luggage but taking them right back to camp. Who can blame him? Seven daughters—he was probably just enjoying being an empty nester and playing golf on Tuesdays. What is even more endearing is the way this mentor approached Moses. He said nothing but embraced him, broke bread with him, heard all the incredible works the Lord had done, celebrating the wins with his son-in-law. What a precious moment as I imagine them laughing, breadcrumbs everywhere, Moses reenacting the story of Pharaoh and the Red Sea victory. Jethro, probably even a little teary-eyed knowing the times he told this forty-year-old "Egyptian" about God when he first moved in decades ago, and now seeing him doing such great work for the Lord—wow!

Then in chapter 18:17–23 you can see how Jethro responded the next morning to seeing Moses leave sunup until sundown, it now becoming painfully obvious what was causing all the stress in his son-in-law's life.

> *[17] "Moses' father-in-law replied, 'What you are doing is not good. [18] You and these people who come to you will only wear yourselves out. The work is too heavy for you; you cannot handle it alone. [19] Listen now to me and I will give you some advice, and may God be with you. You must be the people's representative before God and bring their disputes to him. [20] Teach them his decrees and instructions, and show them the way they are to live and how they are to behave. [21] But select capable men from all the people—men who fear God, trustworthy men who hate dishonest gain—and appoint them as officials over thousands, hundreds, fifties and tens. [22] Have them serve as judges for the people at all times, but have them bring every difficult case to you; the simple cases they can decide themselves. That will make your load lighter, because they will share it with you. [23] If you do this and God so commands, you will be able to stand the strain, and all these people will go home satisfied.'"*

This partnership with Jethro plays a role in Moses's leadership development, and essentially in how the Hebrews would develop themselves as a nation. I can't wait to meet Jethro in heaven. What wisdom he had and what an honor to be used by God to come in and build strategic plans for growth into arenas that Moses had never been before. This is what building something new looks like—we go places we've never gone, we do things we have never done—and it takes mentors, teachers, and wise counsel speaking into our decisions and choices.

Taking Feedback

Jethro came in and spoke truth to the situation that Moses and the Israelites were in. But that was just part of the solution. It was crucial that Moses take his feedback and run with it.

READ EXODUS 18:24-26

> [24] "Moses listened to his father-in-law and did everything he said. [25] He chose capable men from all Israel and made them leaders of the people, officials over thousands, hundreds, fifties and tens. [26] They served as judges for the people at all times. The difficult cases they brought to Moses, but the simple ones they decided themselves."

Moses listened and, together with Jethro, made a plan. He chose leaders from among the people and delegated responsibilities to them. He delegated, deferred, or did it. He allowed them to bring him only the most difficult disputes, but the day-to-day functioning of the nation would no longer rest solely on his shoulders. Jethro's feedback and advice would have been useless if Moses had not taken it to heart, without being defensive. I imagine this was an intentional choice on Moses's behalf. Sometimes it's difficult to not be defensive when someone gives us feedback. But it's clear that Moses respected his father-in-law, and his advice led them forward.

Stronger Together

When we don't know how to set a foundation for our next steps, wisdom teaches us to seek mentors and friends who have walked the path we are walking. It isn't enough just to "hold us up," but sometimes we need someone to say, "I'm with you. We're in this together, and you're going to make it."

What a relief it is to find someone else who has tread difficult ground before us! Sometimes, it feels as if we've done all we can do. Growth requires us to remain (or become) humble in our intentions. We do so by inviting feedback and partnership from those with more experience, vision, and wisdom. These are the people who will help us build and grow.

As we grow, we learn to avoid the pitfalls of impatience, foolishness, and fear that can completely derail our journeys. We build habits of faith that keep us focused on the long game, and we learn to trust God as He guides us every step of the way. Friend, let's leave behind the things that have kept us in slavery, and let's press forward into a life of freedom.

A Prayer

Father, help me to know when I'm approaching burnout. Give me the wisdom and clarity to know when I should be on the battlefield, when I should be leading, and when I should be holding up the arms of others. God, bring wise mentors into my life and keep defensiveness far from me so that I can hear them clearly. Thank You, Lord, for the way that You use Your people to accomplish Your will here on earth. I'm grateful to be Your child.

Questions for Reflection

» I love Jethro's heart to mentor Moses. Have you ever had someone come alongside you when things start to get tired and wearisome? In this coming week, write down a few names of people you'll pray for, thank, and write them a quick note or text about how much their mentorship meant to you.

» My pastor used to say that we should always have three people in our lives: someone pouring into us; a peer, colleague, and friend to be just you; and someone that YOU are pouring into. Do you have a mentee in your life that you are celebrating, pouring into their love bank before offering guidance?

» What things did Jethro do with Moses before he started assessing the situation? (See Ex. 18:7-12.) How can we encourage others today?

» Jethro recognized that Moses's pace was not sustainable. Burnout for leaders is real, y'all. You may be experiencing burnout yourself. I am praying with you, friend, that a Jethro would come into your life. Often, it may even take the courage to step out and find someone to pour into us. Summarize Jethro's advice (18:17-23).

THURSDAY

READ EXODUS 19:1-31

Every structure has a breaking point. That's why roads, bridges, and buildings are designed with what's called a "factor of safety." A factor of safety expresses how much stronger a system is than it needs to be for an intended load. Without this margin when it comes to safety, a system or structure could fail if unexpected stress occurs. The same can be said for humans. Many of us walk around every day with no margin.

An unexpected emergency, season of stress, or even getting caught in traffic can cause our whole schedule (and attitude) to fall apart.

Creating a Strategy for Margin

Moses was about to receive a massive amount of information from the Lord. That information would shape the very fabric of the Israelite nation. But at the beginning of Exodus chapter 18, Moses did not have the margin or capacity to receive it. In order for Moses to play the role he was destined to play, and in order for the nation of Israel to move forward, something had to change.

READ EXODUS 19-31

While you don't need to read this entire text today, I want to encourage you to read it at some point. But for today, simply look through all the headings in your Bible and write down what is happening in these twelve chapters:

What I love about chapter 18 is that it tells us, thanks to Jethro, Moses was free to go hear and from the Lord. This was crucial to moving the story forward and setting in motion everything that was to come for the nation of Israel. Take a moment and jot down your thoughts here. What do you think about Moses before Jethro came versus after? Can you think of a time when you felt like Moses before a Jethro showed up in your life?

A Wise Word of Advice

I was really burnt out in a recent season, and I called a friend of mine who had been experiencing a similar season but was further along the path than I was. She immediately spoke encouragement to my heart.

"Last week I was burnt out, and I didn't know what to do next. I felt the Lord telling me to lay down and rest," she told me. "I wanted to get back to my emails, finalize the campaign posts on social media to align with the recently published newsletter, and a dozen other things. But I kept feeling the Lord call me to take a minute for my mental and physical health and just rest."

She was obedient to the Lord and woke up to two emails with over $60,000 in donations for their capital campaign! God will often provide our needs while we seek Him and His rest.

Moses was burning out. Jethro could see it and had a remedy. And when he was done encouraging and advising Moses, Jethro went home. He didn't try to take over or step in and do it for Moses; he trusted Moses with his daughter, his grandchildren, and the call of God.

Chosen and Set Apart

It was during these next chapters of the book, Exodus 20–31, that Moses received some of the most important words in the Old Testament: the giving of the Ten Commandments, the laws, instructions about the census, the tabernacle, items for the altar, ways for priests to worship, and more. It was God's blueprint for the Hebrews' next season. You can read even more details in Numbers and Leviticus. Moses followed through with many of these directives, including the census in Numbers, which described the two-million-people count and the divvying up of land by tribes.

This is important because it shows that God was making them a unique and separate nation. Remember the Egyptian rituals, customs, pantheon of gods, and caste systems? This is all the Hebrews had known until this point. It would be natural for them to create a copy of where they came from, because they knew it worked. Sometimes it's hard to think beyond what we've known in the past. The Hebrews may have been bound to set up a similar foundation if God had not hand-delivered a new blueprint.

Moses needed time alone to hear from the Lord. He had taken the people as far as he knew how. He knew he needed to do something new to go to the next step. That is entrepreneurship and leadership: to lead and grow further than you've ever been!

If you do what you've always done, you'll end up doing what you always have done. Another way to say it is, "If nothing changes, nothing changes." Think for a moment of how such an attitude could have impacted the children of Israel. The only way they had ever known was the Egyptian way. But God had other plans. And He provided in a special way.

God used Jethro to get them to their next step. But He used Moses's heart to receive feedback and take direction to make change.

Moses needed Jethro to help create a method to allow him time with the Father, where he would receive exact direction for the next season. Moses desperately needed to hear from the Lord to get ready for what was coming next.

Circle in Exodus 31:12–18 the parts that God is highlighting to you in this season.

A Prayer

God thank You that You know exactly what we need when we need it. Thank You that You send people into our lives to help guide and direct us. Thank You that You have many ways You speak to us, including sending others into our lives. Help us to be those blessings to one another, to choose timing wisely, and to be open to ideas that allow for the growth that You want for us. Help our hearts to be open to do things differently if needed. We trust You and know You only want the best for us and to reach all that You have, even if that means making changes. Amen.

Questions for Reflection

» What is your attitude toward correction, criticism, or hard feedback from wise counsel?

» What would you define as wise counsel? Do you think relationship and approach are crucial to receiving correction? Why or why not?

» What does 1 Peter 2:9 say about who YOU are called to be?

» Dwell on Psalm 19 and see what stands out to you now that you have more insight on the varying laws the Old Testament carried.

» Contrast Jesus's time on earth in Hebrews 8:1–10:18 now that you have more knowledge about Exodus's laws.

FRIDAY

The Danger of Old Habits

Take your time while you read Exodus 32:1–35 today. I want to point out a few things about this passage, but first I'd like you to journal some thoughts about what is happening here. The Hebrew people had been through so much and they'd learned so much. What stands out to you the most about this passage?

Do you remember what a bull represented in Egyptian culture? In Egyptian culture (the only culture this generation of Hebrews had known), when someone needed strength, they built a bull and worshiped it. That was the answer. That's the culture this generation of Hebrews grew up in. Need strength? Build a bull.

Moses went up on the mountain to hear from the Lord, but there was so much about that process that was unknown. The Hebrews were just learning what it meant to trust God. They relied heavily on Moses to hear from God and tell them what to do. It was an important step for Moses to leave their presence and go up on the mountain and isolate himself to hear from the Lord, but it meant that he would have to leave someone else in charge of the people while he was gone. This person would have to settle the disputes and keep the peace, with no input from Moses. He needed someone he could trust.

Moses chose his brother Aaron to step into that role, and it didn't take long for the Hebrews to start worrying. What does 32:1 say? After all, no one, not even Moses, knew how long he would be up there. I'm sure murmurs spread through the camp at this point. Where was he? What if he didn't come back? What if they were stranded?

In that moment, Aaron succumbed to the requests of the people, and he chose a way to help quell their fears. It was a familiar way to the people, and the golden calf and celebration surrounding it brought immediate relief. Let's look at the beginning of chapter 32 again as we try to figure out why the Hebrews would behave this way.

> [1] "When the people saw that Moses was so long in coming down from the mountain, they gathered around Aaron and said, 'Come, make us gods who will go before us. As for this fellow Moses who brought us up out of Egypt, we don't know what has happened to him.'
>
> [2] "Aaron answered them, 'Take off the gold earrings that your wives, your sons and your daughters are wearing, and bring them to me.' [3] So all the people took off their earrings and brought them to Aaron. [4] He took what they handed him and made it into an idol cast in the shape of a calf, fashioning it with a tool. Then they said, 'These are your gods, Israel, who brought you up out of Egypt.'
>
> [5] "When Aaron saw this, he built an altar in front of the calf and announced, 'Tomorrow there will be a festival to the LORD.' [6] So the next day the people rose early and sacrificed burnt offerings and presented fellowship offerings. Afterward they sat down to eat and drink and got up to indulge in revelry."

I want to propose here that the culture of the Hebrews' past was still so ingrained, even Aaron's, that they resorted to old behaviors when stress and fear took its toll. *They had no other role models; they were simply doing what they had always known.* It's easy to feel a little bit of frustration or annoyance for the Hebrews' choices at this moment. Why would they build a golden calf after they witnessed the miracle of their very own liberation? Listen, if we were together, I'd turn your shoulders to face me, look you in your eye and slowly say, "they only were doing what they've always known."

Choosing Empathy

Have you ever resorted to old behaviors when fear was staring you in the face? It's important to stop here and be reflective of our empathy for ourselves and for others. I can count multiple times that I see people resort to old behaviors as a form of comfort. I know I have! Old relationships that we know are no good, too much food or too little, drinking to the point of drunkenness, excessive entertainment to numb our minds. We all have had habits and hang-ups that we've relied on from our past and maybe even habits that we want to consider now. Don't be like the children of Israel; you have the choice. You hold the power to choose what you want to lean into when you are afraid, upset, or scared. Start creating a new habit today!

God is patient with our humanity. He knows better than you do how your brain works. He knows what you have inherited spiritually. He also knows what you have inherited in your chemical makeup. He is intimately aware of how the trauma you've experienced in your lifetime has impacted your neurology. He also knows what you haven't learned yet, and He wants to be the one to teach you how to go further than you've ever dreamed.

How can we break away from the repetitive, useless behaviors of our past? God invites us to expand ourselves by reminding us what He is after. God did not require a performative sacrifice to a golden calf; He continually invited the Israelites into trust through acts of obedience through uncertainty. It is our choice to partner with God and others to break our old patterns of thinking and habitual behaviors we've gained through modeling and life experience. We must learn to humbly accept feedback by surrounding ourselves with people who believe in us and our ability to break free from the chains that hold us down.

If you have been around a baby learning to walk, you may remember the moments when the baby takes a couple steps and falls and looks up. And what do we do? We cheer them on, run and grab Mom or Dad and pull out our cameras to capture the moment. Beloved, I want you to picture God doing that with you. Anytime you take a few steps and fall, picture your heavenly Father pulling out His camera to capture the moment, calling the cloud of hosts to come around and cheer you on. Keep going. He knows, friend. He knows. You've got this!

Purpose of the Law

Turn to Deuteronomy 11:13–21. This is considered the Mosaic Covenant, known in Judaic culture as a foundational prayer called the Shema. Why did God make another covenant in addition to the Abrahamic Covenant? "The Mosaic Covenant was a conditional covenant that either brought God's direct blessing for obedience or God's direct cursing for disobedience upon the nation of Israel. Part of the Mosaic Covenant was the Ten Commandments (*Exodus 20*) and the rest of the Law, which contained over 600 commands—roughly 300 positive and 300 negatives. The history books of the Old Testament (Joshua–Esther) detail how Israel succeeded at obeying the Law or how Israel failed miserably at obeying the Law. *Deuteronomy 11:26–28* details the blessing/cursing motif."[1]

A Prayer

Father, thank You for knowing me so intimately. You alone are familiar with all my ways. You know my deepest traumas and the longings of my heart. Thank You for never running out of patience as I learn and grow to trust You. May I extend empathy and grace to others when they rely on old habits for comfort, and may I recognize and have compassion for myself when I do the same. Thank You for never leaving me where You found me, but for walking beside me as I learn and grow.

Questions for Reflection

» What's the hardest part about waiting on the Lord?

» Describe a time when you waited on God and it paid off.

» What are some things you can do while you wait on an answer or breakthrough from the Lord?

» I'm so grateful for God's New Covenant with Jesus (Ephesians 2:8–9), which allows for the fulfillment of the Law. Even with Jesus becoming the ultimate sacrifice for sins and the need for the high priest no longer required, do you still see that obedience to follow God's ways is important (v. 10)?

LESSON SIX

PREPARING FOR THE PROMISE

MONDAY

There once was a man who failed in business at the age of 21. Dreaming of a life in politics and leadership, he ran for office and was defeated in a legislative race at age 22. He decided to try his hand at running a business, which failed when he was 24. He fell in love at 26, and the woman died, which led him to a nervous breakdown at age 27. This man eventually gathered his courage and ran for Congress when he was 34, and for the Senate when he was 45, losing both times. He decided to shoot for the moon at 47 and ran for vice president, and—you guessed it—lost that race. A final bid for the Senate ended in defeat when he was 49. His life appeared to be marked by failure after failure, and yet he persevered. He could have believed the labels and judgments that likely swirled around his reputation. Instead, he ran one more time and was elected president of the United States at age 52. Most don't count his failures when they think of Abraham Lincoln. He stayed the course, and it paid off. President Lincoln's leadership is woven into the fabric of our nation because of such staunch perseverance.

READ EXODUS 23:20-33

What does this passage indicate about the Lord's relationship with His people?

"The Old Testament describes the Promised Land in two ways. In passages like 23:23, it is identified as the land of certain peoples who Israel must destroy. In those like 23:31, it is indicated in general terms by its boundaries. The location of the Promised Land was certain, but its precise extent depended on Israel's faith and commitment to take possession of it. In Joshua and Judges, we find that Israel failed to inherit as much as it might have because of sin and faithlessness. Eventually, the people's unfaithfulness to the covenant led them to forfeit their right to live as an independent state, and they were forced to submit to foreign domination (see 2 Kings 17; Jeremiah 25)."[1]

READ EXODUS 33:1-34:35

This is a long portion of text, but these are crucial moments for Moses and his friendship with God.

» Do you see a subtle shift in Moses's relationship with the Lord? What is happening?

» What do you see Joshua doing?

READ EXODUS 35:20-36:7

I find it fascinating to read God directing the Israelites in building the tabernacle, using their gifts to create a holy place. Friend, God has called you to use your gifts in obedience, too. As you lean in toward His promise, remember what He has taught you. There is always more to learn as we follow His lead! The more we obey and walk in step with the Spirit, He will continue to be faithful. His grace knows no end.

As Exodus concludes, you may not think there was an "ending" like one would expect, but Leviticus and Numbers continue with more details of the laws and direction that Moses and the leaders receive. At last, they are called to enter the land. Then we come to the book of Deuteronomy.

Deuteronomy means "copy" or "repetition" as Moses retells the story that just happened in Exodus while out in the wilderness and gives us additional details as well. Even amidst complaining and rebellion of the people, we continue to see that God was faithful to lead and guide them. And we will see that in the midst of hardship, the blessings of a new generation would arise. As Moses sat on the border of Canaan, what was he thinking? What was his heart longing for?

READ THE LORD'S COMMAND IN DEUTERONOMY 1:34-39 (ESV)

> [34] "And the LORD heard your words and was angered, and he swore, [35] 'Not one of these men of this evil generation shall see the good land that I swore to give to your fathers, [36] except Caleb the son of Jephuneh. He shall see it, and to him and to his children I will give the land on which he has trodden, because he has wholly followed the LORD!' [37] Even with me the LORD was angry on your account and said, 'You also shall not go in there. [38] Joshua the son of Nun, who stands before you, he shall enter. Encourage him, for he shall cause Israel to inherit it. [39] And as for your little ones, who you said would become a prey, and your children, who today have no knowledge of good or evil, they shall go in there. And to them I will give it, and they shall possess it.'"

Here we hear the stern warnings about where rebellion can lead, but we are also assured that the group of people who were raised in the wilderness were going to be strong enough to possess the land. Any mamas reading this right now know that feeling when you see your kids thriving—when you see them pass tests with grace and courage and you are so proud for all that is ahead.

The Israelite kids who grew up in the wilderness were tough. They knew to rely on the Lord. They had no recollection of the pantheon that Egypt admired. They only knew the great I Am and they trusted His ability to provide while learning to hear His voice.

I don't know about you, but I want to reach my promises. I don't want to be compared to oxen—a "stiff-necked people"—and continue to walk in circles learning lesson after lesson, failing over and over. I want to shake off pride and rebellion, murmuring and complaining. I want to be part of the generation that walks the land of promises. I want to refuse the poverty and scarcity mentality and grab hold with all my heart a posture of gratitude, praise, hopeful expectation, trust, and deep conviction to be obedient to His leading. I want to use my gifts for His kingdom here on earth. We've got this, ladies; the future IS ours.

A Prayer

Father, help me to stay the course. Keep me focused on You and Your mighty plan. May I see and hear You clearly and may my walk through the wilderness strengthen me for the road ahead. Thank You for having a plan for me; thank You for walking the path alongside me. I reject pride and rebellion right now, Lord. Give me the strength to persevere. I love You.

Questions for Reflection

» In what ways were the next generation of Israelites who grew up in the wilderness different from their parents?

>> How do you think these attributes would help them as they prepared to walk into the land that was promised to them?

>> Take a moment to list the spiritual gifts the Lord has given to you.

>> Are there any gifts that have developed in the wilderness? Take some time to pray about this and thank God for His faithfulness.

TUESDAY

READ DEUTERONOMY 34 (ESV)

> [1] *"Then Moses went up from the plains of Moab to Mount Nebo, to the top of Pisgah, which is opposite Jericho. And the Lord showed him all the land, Gilead as far as Dan,* [2] *all Naphtali, the land of Ephraim and Manasseh, all the land of Judah as far as the western sea,* [3] *the Negeb, and the Plain, that is, the Valley of Jericho the city of palm trees, as far as Zoar.* [4] *And the LORD said to him, 'This is the land of which I swore to Abraham, to Isaac, and to Jacob, "I will give it to your offspring." I have let you see it with your eyes, but you shall not go over there.'"*

The sun was strong as Moses sat leaning against a rock at the top of Pisgah. He could see Jericho in the distance. The plains stretched out for miles below him, a vast land, golden beneath the rays of the setting sun. He scratched his beard while he pondered the words the Lord had spoken to him. He'd been traveling and leading the people for so long, it was hard to grasp that he was finally laying eyes on the very land God had promised His people when they fled Egypt so many years ago. A new generation had risen up since then, men and women who were unfamiliar with the gods of the Egyptians and the life of slavery that had been a daily reality for their parents. Those children who had grown up in the wilderness would be the ones to walk in the promised land. In his heart Moses knew he would die before the people crossed the borders.

He leaned his head back and sighed deeply. Even now he could remember what it was like as a young man living in the palace. Back then he was looking forward to the life of a diplomat. How differently his life had unfolded. Moses had become a sojourner, a traveler who wandered and worked every day to follow Yahweh. He closed his eyes and thought of how far the Israelites had come, and how God was so faithful to give them what they needed to create a new nation with its own laws and traditions. He thought of the tabernacle they had created—a place where the presence of God could dwell with His people. One day the Israelites would build a vast and beautiful temple in their own land, and the thought brought a smile to his face. He'd done his best to lead God's people out of slavery. He hadn't done the job perfectly, but as he sat on Mount Nebo, he knew in his heart God was pleased, and that was enough. He might never set foot in the promised land, but he'd done the job he had set out to do all those years ago. He opened his eyes and watched the sun begin to fade as he spoke his thoughts aloud to the heavens: *Thank You. Thank You for this life. I'm ready for whatever comes next.*

Moses was approaching the end of his journey. The time of his death was nearing, and I often wonder about his mindset as he reflected on his own path and his hopes for the people. As he thought about the last

40 years of wandering in the desert, he considered the future of the Hebrew people and what it would look like to encounter friends as well as enemies.

We know that Moses talked to the Israelites about what it would look like to encounter other nations and people, and he made an important distinction between two types that would likely move among their camps. He called them sojourners and aliens.

Moses identified strongly with sojourners/foreigners. The Bible tells us he considered himself one. He knew that the people would encounter many who were traveling through, strangers in a strange land, and he was given instructions on how the Israelites were to treat them.

READ DEUTERONOMY 10:18-19 (NLT)

[18] *"He ensures that orphans and widows receive justice. He shows love to the foreigners living among you and gives them food and clothing.* [19] *So you, too, must show love to foreigners, for you yourselves were once foreigners in the land of Egypt."*

READ EXODUS 22:21

"Do not mistreat or oppress a foreigner, for you were foreigners in Egypt."

In other verses, the Lord spoke about non-Israelites. These were not Hebrews but a group of people who had decided to live *with* them permanently. God commanded Moses to tell the Israelites to welcome them. They intermarried, chose to stay and became part of the culture, and they were to have the same rights as the Israelites. They were counted among the two million.

READ DEUTERONOMY 1:16B

> *"Hear the disputes between your people and judge fairly, whether the case is between two Israelites or between an Israelite and a foreigner residing among you."*

READ DEUTERONOMY 24:14-15

> ¹⁴ *"Do not take advantage of a hired worker who is poor and needy, whether that worker is a fellow Israelite or a foreigner residing in one of your towns.* ¹⁵ *Pay them their wages each day before sunset, because they are poor and are counting on it. Otherwise, they may cry to the* Lord *against you, and you will be guilty of sin."*

Sojourner/Foreigner

Gare [H1481]: properly, a guest; by implication, a foreigner; alien, sojourner, stranger.

1. a temporary inhabitant, a newcomer lacking inherited rights
2. of foreigners in Israel, though conceded rights

So, whether they were passing through or choosing to stay, the Lord was clear.

Sometimes we forget that even in the midst of hardship, we can still welcome others to walk with us. We also tend to forget that God often uses the most unlikely characters to bring about His will and play vital roles in our history. People we think would instantly be unqualified to bring about His will are peppered throughout Scripture. Moses is a great example of this: an exiled murderer, who struggled to speak, was used to bring about the great Exodus. God truly can use anyone and everything for His glory. Those who we might consider dismissed and disqualified can rise up beneath His mighty hand. Never count anyone out.

READ DEUTERONOMY 34:5-12 (ESV)

> ^{5} *"So Moses the servant of the* L*ORD* *died there in the land of Moab, according to the word of the* L*ORD,* ^{6} *and he buried him in the valley in the land of Moab opposite Beth Peor; but no one knows the place of his burial to this day.* ^{7} *Moses was 120 years old when he died. His eye was undimmed, and his vigor unabated.* ^{8} *And the people of Israel wept for Moses in the plains of Moab thirty days. Then the days of weeping and mourning for Moses were ended.*
>
> ^{9} *"And Joshua the son of Nun was full of the spirit of wisdom, for Moses had laid his hands on him. So, the people of Israel obeyed him and did as the* L*ORD* *had commanded Moses.* ^{10} *And there has not arisen a prophet since in Israel like Moses, whom the* L*ORD* *knew face to face,* ^{11} *none like him for all the signs and the wonders that the* L*ORD* *sent him to do in the land of Egypt, to Pharaoh and to all his servants and to all his land,* ^{12} *and for all the mighty power and all the great deeds of terror that Moses did in the sight of all Israel."*

Moses, the one who knew God face to face, the leader the Hebrew people had known for 40 years, had died. A chapter in their story had ended, and a new chapter was beginning. Joshua, blessed by Moses, would take up the sword and lead the way. The road would be tough, but they had been strengthened for the journey, and God would go with them.

A Prayer

Father, Your plans for Your people are beyond my comprehension. I am amazed at the way You know us so intimately, and You know what we need at the moment we need it. I trust You, God, as You end certain chapters in my life. Thank You for the path I've walked, and thank You for the way You've strengthened me for the journey. May I embrace the new chapters You set before me. Help me not to forget the lessons You've taught me. Go before me, God, and lead the way. I trust You and I love You.

Questions for Reflection

» As the Israelites grieved the loss of Moses, what are some things they may have feared?

» How do you think Joshua felt as Moses laid hands on him?

» Can you think of a time when God ended a chapter in your life? Take a moment to remember and write down how you felt.

» Looking back, can you see how God worked as He opened a new chapter for you?

» Take some time to pray that you would have eyes to see the hand of God in this season, as you stop walking in circles and break through to the promises God has for you.

WEDNESDAY

I sometimes believe people have this idea that God was giving the children of Israel a giant, empty plot of land in which they would simply reside. There's a misconception that they would begin building houses and cities, complete with irrigation and agriculture. In reality, God was giving the children of Israel the land of Canaan, but Canaan was already a fully established nation that had to be overthrown. God was not just preparing His people in the wilderness for faith; He was preparing them for war. He needed warriors who were going to rely on him, a mighty army that would remember their past. He wanted a group who would go with all their might after the God of Abraham, Isaac, and Jacob.

For decades, the children of Israel had been in a season of bootcamp—emotionally, physically, and spiritually. When they left Egypt, they had no idea that their promise included a conquest and that required training and discipline. Have you found that this is how it often is in God's kingdom?

I have learned that often whatever God has put in your heart will *not* fall into your lap. It will require your co-laboring with God. It can be confusing and disorienting, trying to discern the voice of God. Especially when there are new skills to learn, or things feel a little confusing. For example, in Exodus 14:14, it says, "The LORD will fight for you; you need only to be still." Yet three chapters later, they are told to fight the Amalekites. I wonder if the Israelites were frustrated by seemingly mixed messages. Do we fight or do we stand still? How do we know we're hearing from God clearly? What if we get it wrong?

Discerning what we feel the Lord is saying is not easy for even the most experienced prophetic voices. We must take the time to seek objective evidence that will confirm His commands. We should compare it to Scripture, discuss with other believers whose counsel we trust, and weigh the word against our known facts. The more time you spend listening to the quiet voice of God, hearing His words of confirmation and affection for yourself, the stronger this muscle will become. Your ability to discern grows with each attempt to hear God's voice for yourself.

Leadership Development

In order to take hold of the promise and follow God's lead, we don't just have to learn to hear God's voice; we also have to be willing to grow and develop. It's a process, and if we're doing it right, we will never stop growing. As the Israelites prepared for what came next, God began to develop and strengthen them, specifically in the area of leadership development. Let's take a look at some Scriptures that show different ways the Israelites were strengthened and developed. After each passage, jot down some notes about leadership development.

READ EXODUS 24:13

> *"Then Moses set out with Joshua his aide, and Moses went up on the mountain of God."*

READ NUMBERS 27:12-21

> [12] *"Then the Lord said to Moses, 'Go up this mountain in the Abarim Range and see the land I have given the Israelites.* [13] *After you have seen it, you too will be gathered to your people, as your brother Aaron was,* [14] *for when the community rebelled at the waters in the Desert of Zin, both of you disobeyed my command to honor me as holy before their eyes.' (These were the waters of Meribah Kadesh, in the Desert of Zin.)* [15] *Moses said to the Lord,* [16] *'May the Lord, the God who gives breath to all living things, appoint someone over this community* [17] *to go out and come in before them, one who will lead them out and bring them*

in, so the LORD's people will not be like sheep without a shepherd.' [18] So the LORD said to Moses, 'Take Joshua son of Nun, a man in whom is the spirit of leadership, and lay your hand on him. [19] Have him stand before Eleazar the priest and the entire assembly and commission him in their presence. [20] Give him some of your authority so the whole Israelite community will obey him. [21] He is to stand before Eleazar the priest, who will obtain decisions for him by inquiring of the Urim before the LORD. At his command he and the entire community of the Israelites will go out, and at his command they will come in.'"

READ DEUTERONOMY 1:37-38

[37] "Because of you the LORD became angry with me also and said, 'You shall not enter it, either. [38] But your assistant, Joshua son of Nun, will enter it. Encourage him, because he will lead Israel to inherit it.'"

READ DEUTERONOMY 3:21-29

[21] "At that time I commanded Joshua: 'You have seen with your own eyes all that the LORD your God has done to these two kings. The LORD will do the same to all

> the kingdoms over there where you are going. [22] Do not be afraid of them; the Lord your God himself will fight for you.' [23] At that time I pleaded with the Lord: [24] 'Sovereign Lord, you have begun to show to your servant your greatness and your strong hand. For what god is there in heaven or on earth who can do the deeds and mighty works you do? [25] Let me go over and see the good land beyond the Jordan—that fine hill country and Lebanon.' [26] But because of you the Lord was angry with me and would not listen to me. 'That is enough,' the Lord said. 'Do not speak to me anymore about this matter. [27] Go up to the top of Pisgah and look west and north and south and east. Look at the land with your own eyes, since you are not going to cross this Jordan. [28] But commission Joshua, and encourage and strengthen him, for he will lead this people across and will cause them to inherit the land that you will see.' [29] So we stayed in the valley near Beth Peor."

READ DEUTERONOMY 31:3-8

> [3] "'The Lord your God himself will cross over ahead of you. He will destroy these nations before you, and you will take possession of their land. Joshua also will cross over ahead of you, as the Lord said. [4] And the Lord will do to them what he did to Sihon and Og, the kings of the Amorites, whom he destroyed along with their land. [5] The Lord will deliver them to you, and you must do to them all that I have commanded you. [6] Be strong and courageous. Do not be afraid or terrified because of them, for the Lord your God goes with you; he will never leave you nor forsake you.' [7] Then Moses summoned Joshua and said to him in the presence of all Israel, 'Be strong and courageous, for you must go with this

people into the land that the LORD swore to their ancestors to give them, and you must divide it among them as their inheritance. [8] The LORD himself goes before you and will be with you; he will never leave you nor forsake you. Do not be afraid; do not be discouraged.'"

READ DEUTERONOMY 31:23

"The LORD gave this command to Joshua son of Nun: 'Be strong and courageous, for you will bring the Israelites into the land I promised them on oath, and I myself will be with you.'"

What are some leadership qualities that were displayed in the Scriptures above? Write some of your favorites below:

Giants in the Promised Land

Moses sent a group of men to explore the land. They crept behind enemy lines and came back to report what they'd seen, and there were differing opinions within the group.

READ NUMBERS 13:26-33

> [26] *"They came back to Moses and Aaron and the whole Israelite community at Kadesh in the Desert of Paran. There they reported to them and to the whole assembly and showed them the fruit of the land.* [27] *They gave Moses this account: 'We went into the land to which you sent us, and it does flow with milk and honey! Here is its fruit.* [28] *But the people who live there are powerful, and the cities are fortified and very large. We even saw descendants of Anak there.* [29] *The Amalekites live in the Negev; the Hittites, Jebusites and Amorites live in the hill country; and the Canaanites live near the sea and along the Jordan.'*
>
> [30] *"Then Caleb silenced the people before Moses and said, 'We should go up and take possession of the land, for we can certainly do it.'*
>
> [31] *"But the men who had gone up with him said, 'We can't attack those people; they are stronger than we are.'* [32] *And they spread among the Israelites a bad report about the land they had explored. They said, 'The land we explored devours those living in it. All the people we saw there are of great size.* [33] *We saw the Nephilim there (the descendants of Anak come from the Nephilim). We seemed like grasshoppers in our own eyes, and we looked the same to them.'"*

Although Caleb spoke up and encouraged Moses to move quickly and take possession of the land, the majority of the scouting party disagreed. In fact, all but two of them adamantly refused, using descriptions like *grasshopper* when describing the plight of the Israelites if Moses dared to move against the enemy currently living in the land. This created great terror throughout the people, and they began to grumble and murmur amongst each other, once again doubting God and Moses's leadership. Notice how Moses and Aaron responded:

READ NUMBERS 14:1-4

> [1] *"That night all the members of the community raised their voices and wept aloud. [2] All the Israelites grumbled against Moses and Aaron, and the whole assembly said to them, 'If only we had died in Egypt! Or in this wilderness! [3] Why is the LORD bringing us to this land only to let us fall by the sword? Our wives and children will be taken as plunder. Wouldn't it be better for us to go back to Egypt?' [4] And they said to each other, 'We should choose a leader and go back to Egypt.'"*

Let's stop here and think of how Moses and Aaron could have reacted in this situation. They had developed as leaders, and their hearts in that moment were to turn the people's hearts back toward God and be obedient. They tried as hard as they could to humble themselves and adamantly encourage the people.

READ NUMBERS 14:5-9

> [5] *"Then Moses and Aaron fell face down in front of the whole Israelite assembly gathered there. [6] Joshua son of Nun and Caleb son of Jephunneh, who were among those who had explored the land, tore their clothes [7] and said to the entire Israelite assembly, 'The land we passed through and explored is exceedingly good. [8] If the LORD is pleased with us, he will lead us into that land, a land flowing with milk and honey, and will give it to us. [9] Only do not rebel against the LORD. And do not be afraid of the people of the land, because we will devour them. Their protection is gone, but the LORD is with us. Do not be afraid of them.'"*

Moses and Aaron desperately pleaded with the people. However, the generation that had seen miracle after miracle, from the plagues of Egypt to the parting of the Red Sea, from the manna coming down every morning from heaven to water coming from a rock, refused to trust. And because of that, God proclaimed they would not see the promised land. In the end, only Caleb and Joshua would remain to lead the younger generation against their enemies. It bears saying over and over throughout the Scriptures: Obedience is better than sacrifice (1 Sam. 15:22).

Understand the Past

Egypt was both an arrival and departure. It was both ally and adversary. From Jacob entering due to famine, being blessed and multiplied, to the land that enslaved them for 400 years. And then, it framed the landscape where Moses took them out.

Isn't that how the testimonies of our own bondage can be? It might be where we start and where we exit. It can be the hardest thing we've walked through and the lesson that will launch us into our next season. And often, like all lessons, it requires us putting a microscope to our own hearts, minds, intentions, and character that can, if we let it, shape us into exactly who God needs us to be going forward.

By understanding our past and by learning lessons from our mistakes, we can dream big dreams. By remembering to model our new godly behaviors, we learn to fight and be strengthened by the Spirit. With His help, we can step into all that He has for us. So, dream big, beloved, and jump for the stars. He will catch you.

Joshua had learned about the past by learning from Moses and watching the mistakes of his parents' generation. He had been strengthened in the wilderness. God prepared him for battle, and it was going to take every ounce of cunning and strength he had to pull off the victories that would be required of him. He would have to conquer 31 kings.

Think about that for a moment. Thirty-one kings and their armies stood between the Israelites and the land they had been promised. Joshua had a lot on his plate. He needed to figure out God's strategy and plan to move his people forward, so he sent in spies to help him decide what to do next. This was an important move. And little did he know it would all rest on the shoulders of the most unlikely of allies—a prostitute.

A Prayer

Father, thank You for the way You want to develop us as leaders. Thank You for patiently guiding us into the things we've been destined for. You already know the giants that are in the land ahead of us. Would You go before us, Father, and make a way? Would You speak courage to our hearts and resolve to our minds as we prepare for battle? May we be of good courage. May we never discount someone because of our first impressions of them. May we see You work in mighty and unexpected ways as You free us from the things that hold us back from Your promises. Amen.

Questions for Reflection

» What are some of your favorite leadership qualities from this chapter of Exodus? Pick one and write it in your journal. Pray about how God would develop that quality in you this week.

» Have you ever faced a "giant" obstacle? What did you do? Maybe you're facing one now. Can you model anything you've learned in this chapter to help you overcome it?

THURSDAY

READ JOSHUA 2:1-21

Here we are at the point in the story that we've all been waiting for. The Israelites were fortified, ready. They had been waiting and hearing and preparing for this moment. They sent their spies into the city and then waited to hear what they would find.

"Canaan at this time was not a unified political entity. Instead, it was made up of many small 'kingdoms'—city-states, usually including a major fortified city plus the small villages and farms in the region. Each such city-state would have its own king and its own army."[2]

If you're familiar with this story at all, you've likely heard of Rahab. Rahab was a prostitute, yes, but there is even more that we can deduct from her life based on other parts of Scripture. She owned a brothel that was located near the gates on the wall—a strategic location! I also love her boldness to step in during this once-in-a-lifetime encounter with the Israelites. She pivoted quickly and strategically.

When you read the Scripture, you see that the city was in a state of terror. This is great intel for the spies. If the city was not at all concerned and had the best chariots ready to go, Joshua's response may have been drastically different. But Rahab expressed how everyone in the city had heard of them and had been talking about how the Lord dried up the water at the Red Sea. The battles the Israelites had won and the armies they'd defeated were the talk of the town.

Spies in the ancient Near East regularly collected information about enemy movements and troop sizes. It would not be unusual for spies to infiltrate the enemy forces by posing as deserters or refugees. In reconnoitering a city, they would collect intel regarding defenses, food and water supply, the number of fighting men, and the general preparedness for attack or siege. Most important for the spies was to find out everything they could about the source of the water supply. If the city's water could be cut off or compromised, a siege would have a much better chance of success.[3]

Jericho was a fortified city that sat on a mound, high enough to see the Israelites at camp. The historical site of Jericho is located in eastern Palestine, in what is known as Tell es-Sultan. It relied heavily on the Jordan river for water, and during this specific time of year, Canaanites had finished harvesting and the Jordan river was in the flooding season.

Everyone had seen and heard about the Israelites' god *Yahweh*. Even though these people surely were polytheistic, they feared the Israelites' army. I love how this had changed in the last four decades. Remember when Moses asked who he should say sent him and God answered, "I AM WHO I AM" (Ex. 3:13–14). Now all the kids on the block knew His name! Including Rahab.

"The report the Canaanites have heard suggests that he can influence the weather as well as bodies of water, disease and the animal world. Though her confession expresses how impressed they all are with the range of Yahweh's authority and power, it is far from an expression of monotheism. She has neither renounced her gods nor offered to dispose of them. She has not affirmed any loyalty to Yahweh but has requested his help. She shows no knowledge of the obligations of the law, and we have no reason to think she is aware of the revolutionary religious system that was developing in Israel. In short, her speech does not suggest that she has risen much above her polytheistic perspective—but she knows power when she sees it."[4]

If you're anything like me, I can picture this as a movie scene in my head. I imagine a scene from *Troy*, you know the one with Brad Pitt in 2004, where they all have to sneak into the Trojan horse because of the fortified city. Here in Jericho it was giant rock walls with stone stairs and a cobblestone window. The spies peeked out from underneath the hay while Rahab answered the door and, in her Oscar-winning performance, sent the soldiers on a wild goose chase to take advantage of this one shot to save her family.

As soon as the soldiers left, she helped lower the spies down and then ran frantically through the city to find her family. They bundled into the house that night, and once she was sure all of her loved ones were inside safely, she crept up to the window. She likely saw the glowing lights from the Israelites' camp, sending shivers up her spine. Then, she ever so carefully hung her scarlet cord from her window. I like to think she said a little prayer under her breath, trusting God and the Israelites enough to uphold their end of the bargain.

"Rahab asks boldly and receives the fruit of her faith. When the city is under siege from fire and rampaging soldiers, Rahab gathers her family members into her own home and transforms her scarlet letter into a scarlet cord of protection. Symbolically, the rope by which she lets the spies down from her window becomes a flare of hope when they return to conquer the city. Rahab's cord transforms her status as a lady in red into a lady in waiting to the King of Kings."[5]

This is not the first time we have seen women face fear with courage during this study. Think about the Hebrew midwives not giving in to man's decree but having a fear of the Lord. Or Moses's mother Jochebed and sister Miriam seeing something special and not giving in to the deadly decree. Even Pharaoh's daughter refused her father's decree, and instead followed the prompting of her heart. Here we see another woman of courage stepping up and changing history. Rahab feared God more than man and hid the spies from the soldiers of Jericho.

Soon, the Israelites could be heard marching toward the city, the ark of the covenant on display for all to see. All of Jericho was watching in a panic, no one coming or going. As the priests stepped in the swift and swollen Jordan river, once again the waters formed a wall and everyone below them was cut off. The knowledge of it rippled through the city—Yahweh was with the Hebrews yet again (Josh. 3:14–17).

READ JOSHUA 6:22-23 (NLT)

> [22] *"Meanwhile, Joshua said to the two spies, 'Keep your promise. Go to the prostitute's house and bring her out, along with all her family.'*
> [23] *"The men who had been spies went in and brought out Rahab, her father, mother, brothers, and all the other relatives who were with her. They moved her whole family to a safe place near the camp of Israel."*

Ladies, it's time to take off your scarlet letter and hang it in the window. The Lord is coming, and He wants to use your past for greatness. He doesn't care what you have been through or where you come from.

Stand up in faith. Look fear in the face and step forward with courage. Yahweh, in His mercy and strength, will lead you on.

A Prayer

Lord God, You are so faithful. Thank You for the story of Rahab and other courageous women of the Bible. Thank You for choosing the most unlikely people to join you and Your mighty plans. May I have courage and faith to see what is possible when I choose Your ways. May future generations be blessed because I have chosen to follow You. You are so good. Thank You for loving me.

Questions for Reflections

» Have you ever risked trusting someone with something important? Why did you trust them? What did you learn from that experience?

» What qualities or traits helped Rahab partner with the spies of Israel?

» Which quality of Rahab is your favorite? Why?

» How did this quality or trait help Rahab and her family survive?

FRIDAY

For six weeks we've walked with the Israelites as they moved from slavery into the freedom God had promised them. Hopefully, you feel like you know them better. Maybe you understand why they made the choices they made, and why God led them the way He did. I know it can seem like the Israelites wandered in circles for 40 years. But they didn't.

The stories we read in the book of Exodus take place over a 13-month period of time. Read that again. Thirteen months. From the time they fled Egypt to the time they made it to Mount Sinai and were given the law and the blueprints for the tabernacle, only 12 months had passed. Then, the book of Leviticus, where Moses received more instructions, was only a 30-day timespan, leaving us with 13 months.

In Numbers, which literally is Hebrew for "wilderness," the Israelites get direction from God to leave Mount Sinai after 13 months. We see in Numbers chapter 2 the Lord told Moses to take a census and organize the people by tribe, clan, and family, and to build the tabernacle. On the east side of the tabernacle were the tribes Judah, Issachar, and Zebulon (186k). South were Gad, Simeon, and Rueben (151k). Gathered to the west were Ephraim, Manasseh, and Benjamin (108k), and to the north were Naphtali, Asher, and Dan (157k).

Two million people were finally organized and, on the move, the covenant had been reaffirmed, the law had been given, and the tabernacle had been built. Dr. Bill Creasy, my favorite professor, says "By (Numbers) chapter five they knew who they were, where they belonged, and what they were supposed to do." I love the picture of identity here.

The Israelites were getting tired of being in such close quarters, and by Numbers chapter 6 God offered them a Nazarite vow, which allowed them to separate from community and seek the Lord. Only three people in the Bible have taken the lifelong Nazarite vows (Samson, Samuel, and John the Baptist).

By the end of Numbers chapter 10, it had been two years, two months, and 20 days. We have the ability to see the story from beginning to end, so we know they spent 40 years in the wilderness. But the Israelites had no clue they would "wander" the desert for 38 more years.

If you reference a map, you can see the fastest route as they leave Mount Sinai is to follow the King's Highway up to Raban, where it converges with the Via Maris (the two largest trade routes in antiquity). This crossroads was controlled by the Edomites. Moses went to the King of Edom and asked permission to pass (Num. 20:14–21) and was refused.

So two million Israelites, who were incredibly hungry and thirsty yet again, found an oasis at Kadesh-Barnea. They set up camp and remained there for the next 37 years.

It's important to note that the Israelites would not take possession of the trade routes of Via Maris and the King's Highway until much later under King David's rule when "David takes a loose confederation of twelve tribes and forges a monarchy to take possession of the trade route," says Creasy. What many may not realize is that David's entire reign was fighting a war. Let that sink in. If you had any doubts that going to battle is part of the promises of God, this is evidence to the contrary.

After 37 years in Kadesh-Barnea and one more attempt to cross that met with another refusal by Edom, many Israelites had died a natural death. As we've learned, this new generation of Hebrews had been hardened by the wilderness and they'd learned to hear God's voice and trust Him. They were led by Joshua and Caleb, who had shown the faith and determination to lead them where they needed to go.

Moses said, "Enough already," and they departed again, this time through the south, through Moab, and the plains of Jericho. They made camp on the banks of Canaan. It was finally time, after waiting 40 years, that see their Rahab moment.

Looking back on our time together through Exodus, I've come up with some significant milestones we've encountered along the way. Feel free to look back at your notes and add some of your own:

» Identity

» Consecration

» Gifts and character strengthened

» Not giving up

» Learning new ways to fight battles

» Spiritual warfare

Do you see how all the things listed above are required to go after your promises? Can you see how these things take time and the perfect planning of a good and loving Father? Maybe the Israelites weren't just walking around in dizzy circles for 40 years. Maybe God was taking them the long route through the desert because it was the only way they would really enter the promised land with the character and strength necessary to thrive.

Is it possible this is also true for you, friend?

Maybe this whole time you thought you were walking in circles, not hearing Him, but God is actually carefully positioning you exactly where He wants you to develop all the things you need to reach your promises. It might be taking longer than you thought it would, but in the end you will understand.

Intimacy with God and a meaningful life of purpose can be found on the journey between slavery and the promised land.

A Prayer

During our study I have written prayers to help you find your way through Exodus. I'd love for our last prayer to be one that I prayed over you as I wrote this study.

Father, thank You for this journey You've allowed us to walk together. Would you strengthen my sisters to understand who they are in You? Would You envelop them in Your peace and help them to feel Your good and perfect intentions for them? And when they're feeling empty and stuck, Lord, would You encourage their hearts and remind them that You are with them? Thank You for Your grace and mercy; thank You for your provision as we move forward. Empower us to walk in Your ways with courage. In Jesus's name, Amen.

ACKNOWLEDGMENTS

WOW, THIS BOOK has been something I've been stewing on and studying for many, many years. I am grateful to Professor David Howard from Bethel Seminary, who allowed me to do my independent exegesis under him and gave great insight and wisdom. Thank you to copywriter Mandy Capehart for helping me take all my ideas and get them straightened out and cohesive. Special thanks and shout out to my friend, colleague, and writer extraordinaire Jenna Benton, who was so gracious to drop it all and fly out to help me push this over the finish line. What a great team of talented individuals who showed up and brought their incredible gifts for us all to learn and grow from.

Thank you, Auntie Retta and Uncle Gerry, for helping me get through seminary and sparking my love for the Word while in rehab.

As always, I want to thank my husband and kids for their patience and grace while we ate take-out many nights and sacrificed weekend outings exploring our new city, so that I could finish my word count. Now, let's celebrate!

Lastly, my Nannie Phyllis, you prayed me here. Never underestimate the power of a praying grandma!

BIBLIOGRAPHY

Blank, Wayne. "Wilderness Journey." *Daily Bible Study—Amon of Judah.*
Accessed October 04, 2016. http://www.keyway.ca/htm2002/wildjour.htm.

Burke, Jonathan (Jon), et al. "The Historicity of the Exodus." The BioLogos
Forum, February 23, 2016, discourse.biologos.org/t/the-historicity-of-the
-exodus/4468/24

Buttrick, George A., ed. *The Interpreter's Bible*, vol. 1. Nashville: Abingdon
Press, 1984.

Creasy, Bill. *Exodus Bible Study.* E-book, ed. Logos Bible Study, 2011.

Creasy, Bill. "Gunfight at The OK Corral, Part 1" Logos Bible Study, Lesson
#5. https://www.scribd.com/presentation/227397173/5-Gunfight-at-the
-OK-Corral-Part-1

Creasy, Bill. "Gunfight at The OK Corral, Part 2" Logos Bible Study, Lesson
#6. https://www.scribd.com/presentation/227397266/6-Gunfight-at-the
-OK-Corral-Part-2

Cole, R. A. *Exodus: An Introduction and Commentary.* Downers Grove, IL:
InterVarsity, 1973.

Eddie. "The Historicity of the Exodus." *The BioLogos Forum.* February 23,
2016. Accessed October 04, 2016. https://discourse.biologos.org/t/the
-historicity-of-the-exodus/4468/20

Elwell, W. A., and Barry J. Beitzel. *Baker Encyclopedia of the Bible.* Grand
Rapids: Baker, 1997.

Elwell, W. A., and Barry J. Beitzel. "Plagues upon Egypt." *Baker Encyclopedia
of the Bible*, vol. 2. Grand Rapids: Baker, 1988.

Enns, Peter. *Exodus: NIV Application Commentary: From Biblical Text . . .
to Contemporary Life.* Grand Rapids: Zondervan, 2000.

Exodus, LifeChange Bible Study. Colorado Springs: NavPress, 2018 ed.

GotQuestions.org. "What Are the Covenants in the Bible?" *GotQuestions.org*, October 28, 2003, www.gotquestions.org/Bible-covenants.html

Jakes, T. D. *God's Leading Lady*. New York: Berkley Publishing, 2003.

Katz, Arthur. *Apostolic Foundations: The Challenge of Living an Authentic Christian Life*. Laporte, MN: Burning Bush Publications, 1999.

LaSor, William Sanford, David Allan Hubbard, and Frederic William. *Old Testament Survey: The Message, Form, and Background of the Old Testament*. Grand Rapids: Wm. B. Eerdmans, 1982.

Matthews, V. H., M. W. Chavalas, and J. H. Walton. *The IVP Bible Background Commentary: Old Testament*. Vol. 2. Downers Grove, IL: InterVarsity Press, 2000.

McFadden, Christopher. "Which of the Ancient Egyptian Gods Were the Most Important?" *Interesting Engineering*. June 12, 2019. Accessed June 2021. https://interestingengineering.com/which-of-the-ancient-egyptian-gods-were-the-most-important

Oswalt, John N. *Cornerstone Biblical Commentary: Exodus*. Vol.1. Carol Stream, IL: Tyndale House Publishers, 2005.

Palmer, Parker J. *Let Your Life Speak: Listening for the Voice of Vocation*. San Francisco: Jossey-Bass, 2000.

Stuart, Douglas K. *Exodus: The New American Commentary*. Nashville: Broadman & Holman Publishers, 2006.

Swanson, J. and O. Nave. *New Nave's Topical Bible*. Oak Harbor, WA: Logos Research Systems, 1994.

Then and Now Bible Map Book. Torrance, CA: Rose Publishing, 2005.

Walton, John H. *Ancient Near Eastern Thought and the Old Testament*. Grand Rapids: Baker Academic, 2017.

Walton, John H. and J. Harvey Walton. *The Lost World of the Israelite Conquest*. Downers Grove, IL: IVP Academic, 2017.

NOTES

Lesson 1: Remember the Promise

1. John Walton and J. Harvey Walton, *The Lost World of the Israelite Conquest* (Downers Grove, IL: IVP Academic, 2017), 8–10.
2. https://interestingengineering.com/which-of-the-ancient-egyptian-gods -were-the-most-important
3. https://en.wikipedia.org/wiki/Via_Maris#cite_note-2

Lesson 2: Remember Who YOU Are

1. Arthur Katz, *Apostolic Foundations: The Challenge of Living an Authentic Christian Life* (Laporte, MN: Burning Bush Publications, 1999.)
2. V. H. Matthews, M. W. Chavalas, and J. H. Walton, *The IVP Bible Background Commentary: Old Testament* (electronic ed. Ps. 90:10) (Downers Grove, IL: InterVarsity Press, 2000).

Lesson 3: Remember Who HE Is

1. W. A. Elwell and B. J. Beitzel, "Plagues upon Egypt," in *Baker Encyclopedia of the Bible* (vol. 2) (Grand Rapids: Baker, 1988), 1699.
2. *Matthew Henry's Commentary on the Whole Bible: Complete and Unabridged in One Volume*, 106.
3. Elwell and Beitzel, *Baker Encyclopedia of the Bible*, 1997.
4. Bill Creasy, *Gunfight at the OK Corral, Part 1*.
5. Bill Creasy, *Gunfight at the OK Corral, Part 2*.
6. http://www.stat.rice.edu/~dobelman/Dinotech/10_Egyptian_gods_10 _Plagues.pdf
7. John N. Oswalt, ed., *Cornerstone Biblical Commentary: Exodus* (vol. 1) (Carol Stream, IL: Tyndale House Publishers, 2005), 378.

8. Parker J. Palmer, *Let Your Life Speak: Listening for the Voice of Vocation* (San Francisco: Jossey-Bass, 2000).

9. https://en.wikipedia.org/wiki/King%27s_Highway_(ancient)#/media /File:Ancient_Levant_routes.png

10. Oswalt, *Cornerstone Biblical Commentary*, 5.

11. Ibid., 369.

Lesson 4: Remember Your Strength

1. Ibid., 382.

2. Douglas K. Stuart, *Exodus*, The New American Commentary (Nashville: Broadman and Holman, 2006), 323.

3. Ibid., 297.

4. Ibid., 322.

5. Oswalt, 383.

6. Ibid.

7. Oswalt, 288.

8. Ibid., 388.

9. Ibid.

10. Peter Enns, *Exodus: NIV Application Commentary: From Biblical Text . . . to Contemporary Life* (Grand Rapids: Zondervan, 2000), 273.

11. Stuart, 336.

12. Oswalt, 390.

13. Enns, 278.

14. Oswalt, 389.

Lesson 5: Remembering Your Why

1. https://www.gotquestions.org/Bible-covenants.html

Lesson 6: Preparing for the Promise

1. *Exodus*, in the LifeChange NavPress Bible study series.

2. Matthews, Chavalas, and Walton, *The IVP Bible Background Commentary: Old Testament* (electronic ed., Josh. 2:3). (Downers Grove, IL: InterVarsity Press, 2000).

3. Ibid. (electronic ed., Josh. 2:2).

4. Ibid. (electronic ed., Josh. 2:11).

5. T. D. Jakes, *God's Leading Lady* (New York: Putnam, 2002), 192.

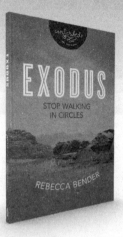

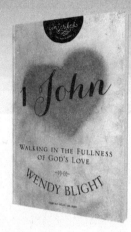

EXODUS (new)

Stop Walking in Circles and Reach God's Destination for Your Life

Rebecca Bender

In this study, Rebecca takes you straight into the book of Exodus where the Israelites are wandering after their own tracks immediately after escaping from bondage and oppression at the hands of Pharaoh. God is trying to get them to the land of his promise, but they, like many of us, are frustrated by doubts, fears, and self-destructive habits.

1 JOHN (new)

Walking in the Fullness of God's Love

Wendy Blight

In this in-depth study of the book of 1 John, Wendy shares the unique insights and wisdom of the last disciple to walk with Jesus. Wendy wrote this book for every woman longing to live out God's unconditional love.

Coming Soon

ChurchSource.com/Inscribed